Ted McRoberts:
NORTH COUNTRY MARSHAL

Ted McRoberts:
NORTH COUNTRY MARSHAL

by Ted McRoberts
As told to Gene Medaris

Great Northwest Publishing
and Distributing Co., Inc.
Anchorage, Alaska
1986

IN DEDICATION

To my wife, Jane,
who has always encouraged
me to write

and

to my two children, Gina and Tim,
who patiently listened to me
read these pages and became
my best critics

INTRODUCTION

Having first come to the Great Land in January 1947, I saw Alaska the way it was when Ted McRoberts lived it as a Deputy U.S. Marshal. Many things were more difficult then. Roads were not very good, clothing often seemed inadequate and travel was tedious—Pan American Airways took over eight hours from Weeks Field to Seattle. Fairbanks reached 10,000 in the summer and about one-half that size in the winter. Gambling, booze and Fourth Avenue women were part of the reputation of this Golden Heart city. Most homes heated with coal or wood and prices were always high. The "bush" was even more difficult.

To change this lifestyle in any manner made enemies of someone, yet, for more than fifty years Ted McRoberts has walked tall in this land. Friend of Washington personalities from Bob Bartlett to Ted Stevens, McRoberts is still loved and remembered for his honesty, integrity and cool-headed manner. Prisoners became his friends and many are now upstanding citizens who remember "The Marshal" as a "good" man. This book is about a living legend, not to those who expeienced the frienship of this remarkable man, but to those who stood at a distance and measured his accomplishments.

ACKNOWLEDGEMENTS

The Journalism Department of the University of Alaska has produced many writers in the past twenty years. Many of these writers thank Jimmy Bedford and Charles Keim for helping them to unleash a desire. A desire to write, which often lies dormant because we do not believe in ourselves. I am no different in this respect.

In 1973, my friend Jimmy Bedford saw some of my writing and made me an offer. "Gene," he said, "if you will take Chuck Keim's 'Magazine Article Writing' course it won't cost you a dime. If you don't sell enough articles to pay for the course, I'll pay for it." How could I lose? But Jimmy didn't have to pay, for Chuck's tutelage produced the best in his students.

Charles Keim became a friend and an inspiration in the months and years following my first journalism course. He believed in me and believed in the story of Ted McRoberts. The result was more than just this book. I got a journalism degree, and became a newspaper editor for four years. I have also published numerous articles and write a newspaper column for the Fairbanks Daily Newsminer.

To acknowledge the contribution of these two men to this book is only a small part of their great contribution to Alaska journalism and the students who owe them so much. The "Chuck and Jimmy Show" still goes on in the lives of their former students.

FOREWORD

BY

U.S. SENATOR TED STEVENS

Ted McRoberts was a tremendous U.S. Marshal, and is a great Alaskan. He epitomized the pioneer spirit that has made Alaska what it is today—the spirit of frontier charity and bush justice. Ted marshaled federal law in our state through the time when few Alaskans understood the need for modern law enforcement techniques, and yet was respected and admired for his fairness and dedication. His insights on life in the bush and the adaptation of American concepts of law to the traditional fairness of native Alaskan cultures illustrate the rich mixture of heritages Alaska shares.

From the time Ted McRoberts set foot in Alaska until now has been barely fifty years—yet the changes that the State has gone through have been staggering. Tourism, fisheries, and oil have replaced logging and mining as Alaska'a preeminent industries. Anchorage, a frontier gateway to the mining country in 1935, has grown into a modern international city—yet the frontier spirit and attitude that Ted McRoberts characterizes so well have not been lost.

Gene Medaris's book brings back a flood of memories—I was privileged to work with Ted McRoberts in Fairbanks during Alaska's last days as a territory. People like Ted McRoberts made miners, trappers, GIs, and new "frontiersmen" alike understand that Alaska would become a state sooner if all agreed the law would be obeyed—and that all offenders would face swift and just retribution for violations.

Ted McRoberts was one of Alaska's great marshals. The tales told of his achievements, and the development of Alaska that he not only witnessed but contributed to, could well be the subject of a TV series to rival those about the old west.

CONTENTS

CHAPTER I

CALL OF THE GREAT LAND

I guess the three of us walking along the docks in Seattle looked like any three men along the docks of any seaport during that late depression year of 1935. Grover Cofelt, Ted "Mac" McAdams and I looked with hungry eyes at the huge ships tied in their berths taking on cargo.

"One of these ships is going to Alaska," I commented, "but how are we going to find out which one?"

"Maybe we ought to just ask," Mac said matter-of-factly as he walked toward a longshoreman struggling to move a crate.

"Say, friend, would you happen to know which of these ships is loading for Alaska?"

"Yea, this one and the second one down there," the worker replied without looking up.

As we walked into the company office to seek passage, I felt for my billfold. The $55 I had saved while tending camp for a sheepherder in Idaho really seemed like a lot of money as I recounted each bill for the hundredth time.

The ship was leaving for Ketchikan the next day; she could carry three passengers. The fare was $50. Elated with the prospects of getting underway, being broke didn't seem to matter much to me now.

The letter I had in my coat pocket from Ethyl Sneed in Ketchikan assured me a new gold rush was starting in Alaska. The coastal areas, which depend chiefly upon fishing, were grievously hurt by the Great Depression of the 1930's, but the gold mining regions were booming. Ethyl's glowing account of life in the great land up north assured me I had only to travel north of the fifty-fourth parallel to find a land of "milk and honey" for anyone willing to work. I was no stranger to work. All that remained was the passage, which I now purchased with the dollars so carefully saved.

I lay in my bunk in the tiny stateroom of the Alaska-bound freighter listening to the sounds coming through the open porthole. The rumble of the city noise, the creaking of cranes lifting cargo, the yelling of dock hands all sang in harmony to the dreams that crowded reality as I lay thinking of the land up north. The deep-throated blast of a ship's horn interrupted the sounds outside. A full minute passed before I realized the sound had come from the ship I was on. We were getting underway!

The slow voyage to Ketchikan was breathtaking. Calm waters soon became the Inside Passage. To me and my two companions, the beauty seemed another omen of assurance that the land ahead was all the letter said it was.

Ketchikan crowded to the sea with lush forests extending into the sunrise over the mountains behind the town, not unlike the logging towns I had seen in my native Idaho. Yet this logging town was something special to me—Alaska's southern gateway to the future seemed to be my gateway, too. I found myself longing, even muttering aloud to Grover and Mac, that I wished the Captain would hurry our slow moving ship into port.

As the freighter docked to unload cargo, and those passengers who had only $50 to ship in Seattle, I walked down the steps of the gangplank, across the wooden wharf and stood on Alaskan soil. A strange feeling for a stranger in a strange land, I guess, but I felt a sense of *belonging* in this new country. I breathed deeply and started to walk toward town— heady with the feeling that at last I was in the land up north.

My childhood friend, Ethyl Sneed, who had written me such positive claims for Alaska's opportunities was a freelance writer in Ketchikan. I decided I should find her first; perhaps she knew of a place to live and maybe a job to go with the last five dollars I had in this world.

Her company was pleasant and the girl with whom I had attended grade school talked as excitedly about the challenge of Alaska as she had written. The excitement of being in the land of a long-time dream, and the thrill that often comes with first experiences, was short-lived. McAdams came running from the docks, right down the middle of the dirt street for he didn't know which house I had entered, yelling, "Ted, Ted, where are you Ted?" I could feel the urgency of his yells and ran into the street to meet my partner who had delivered the letter to the sheep camp that started us travelling together.

"Whoa Mac, just a minute, what's going on that is this good?" I said, trying to slow things down enough to get the message he obviously had on his mind.

Out of breath, McAdams half whispered to me, "Ted, I just found out the *S.S. Yukon* is leaving for Seward in two hours. I've got enough money left for both of us to get passage—last class, but passage."

"What about Cofelt?" I asked.

"He's got money and has alredy bought his passage."

We walked into the house, and I introduced Mac and Ethyl. Mac's excitement was catching and in almost the same breath I said, "We gotta go. Mac says there's a boat leaving and he has money for us to make it." We said goodbye to the girl who had started this northern adventure for us and hurried to the docks to find the agent for the *S.S. Yukon*.

We soon found the office and the rotund little man sitting behind a huge wooden desk. He looked at us with an air of superiority—surely recognizing us as Idaho greenhorns—then lowered his eyes to a passenger manifest. His fingers moved slowly across the list of names before he spoke.

"We have passage in the steerage section, it's the cheapest, if you want that."

McAdams laid the money before the man without a word, neither he nor I would admit that we did not know what section the agent was talking about.

The unknown term was soon explained to us as we were escorted to our quarters. We were led down one flight of stairs, then another and another, until we were deep in the hold of the ship.

"You mean there are staterooms down here?" I whispered to Mac as the old salt led us deeper into the ship.

17

My whisper must have been louder than I thought for the guide chuckled and said, "Only the best on boards, mate." He pointed to a closed door and walked away.

As I opened the door to what I thought was our stateroom, I stepped back in surprise; inside were 500 Filipinos crowded together in the section the agent casually had called "steerage." We vowed to use a dictionary next time before purchasing a ticket if we didn't know what the word meant.

"Oh well," I said to Mac as philosophically as I could, "the trip from Seattle was calm enough, surely the protected passage will be calm, too. This shouldn't be too bad." But then I couldn't know what was soon to happen on the *S.S. Yukon*.

As we left Ketchikan, I noticed the sun seemed to be on the wrong side of the ship if we were heading north. I thought little more about the direction of the sun until we turned into what I later found out was "Dixon Entrance," and the open water of the North Pacific. The ship was heading straight across the Gulf of Alaska!

An hour out of Dixon Entrance the wind began to roll the surface of the ocean into great mountains of white-topped water. The *S.S. Yukon*, big though she was, resembled a fishing cork bobbing on a choppy lake. All hatches were ordered closed. The smell of 500 unbathed men—now it was 502—would have been more than enough to endure in the stale air of the bottom hold. But people began getting sick! One by one, people began to vomit with no place to dispose of the waste. I felt the clammy cold sweat on my brow and the uneasiness rising in my stomach. If just one breath of fresh air were available, maybe, just maybe, I could avert the impending disaster; the latched porthold was the only possibility. Standing for a moment to steady my footing on the rolling deck, I staggered toward the tiny window and grasped the latch as the ship lurched in a yawing roll. As the stern responded to the rising bow, the added force of gravity enabled me to pull the handle downward and open the iron-framed glass that offered the air I now craved so desperately. However, when the window opened, the ship lunged forward again, just as a wall of water broke broadside on the *S.S. Yukon*. Water gushed through the open port with such force that it knocked me to the floor. Scrambling to close the open hole that seemed sure to sink the ship, I made a choice I still remember: seasickness was better than drowning—though I'm still not sure by how much.

Managing to get topside without being seen (we had been ordered to remain below deck), I found a sheltered place on deck and rode out the storm. The cold air and salt spray chilled me to the bone, but anything seemed better than the smell of that room called *steerage* I had left below.

The storm soon passed and the big ship began to move gracefully toward the port of Seward. A spirit of gaiety and entertainment gripped us all, but especially the men returning to work the fishing boats and canneries along the southern coast of Alaska. As the smell of land mingled with the salt, singing and music became spontaneous expressions of happiness. Old miners, with their faces wrinkled and leathery, joined us wide-eyed newcomers in expressions of unrestrained joy. They acted and talked aʳ if Alaska would be the arms of their lover waiting to greet them on   ⁻ᵏₛ of Seward.

The   ꞓ ;outhern Alaska in bathed the freshness of the
'om Idaho walked along the busy dirt street.
minus of the Alaska Railroad, was a busy place
ꞓying cargo for civilian and military needs in
in felt the same excitement I had in Ketchikan
n I first stepped on Alaskan soil—a feeling of
felt before meeting this land.

'ner of the street running from the docks, a man
my eye. He appeared to have stepped from
. novel. The heavy, red beard was streaked
ₑred his face. He was a large man, over six
ᵤ shoulders that stretched against his red flannel
shirt. He wore a sweat-stained felt hat with no headband and pulled the brim down near his eyes. His boots were laced to just below his knees, and dried mud was caked half their length. A smile creased his face as he approached us and we smiled back.

"Howdy," he said, crossing to the other side of the street. The friendliness of this storybook man caused me to turn and call to him.

"Say, friend, could you tell us the best way to get to Anchorage from here?"

"Well, shore I can," he said as he turned to come toward us. "You can walk, you can fly, you can even swim if you don't mind cold water, but if you want to save your money and still ride there is another way."

Cofelt had enough money for his passage to Anchorage, and Mac figured he probably had enough too, but the $5 I had left after my ticket purchase in Seattle had dwindled to only pocket change.

"Listen, fellows, if you have a mind to it I'll tell you how I go to Anchorage," the big man continued. "About eight miles out of town the train must climb a long grade and near the top it slows enough a fellow can 'hook it' if he wants."

McAdams was reluctant and Cofelt just flat refused. I had been reared in a railroad section camp as my father worked building bridges for the railroad in Idaho. I had caught slow moving trains many times as a boy and once travelled from Portland, Oregon to Boise, Idaho when I was about as broke as I was in Seward. At last I convinced Mac it really wasn't difficult to do; he agreed to try.

We thanked our helpful friend and started for the rail station and the eight-mile walk. Luggage wasn't a problem for me. I had been given a slab of bacon and a piece of canvas by a steward on the S.S. Yukon. Tucking these items of worldly wealth under my arm, I walked toward the long grade outside of town with Mac a reluctant two steps behind. Half way up the gradual rise of the grade, we heard the train whistle in the distance and ran to a point near the top where I kept assuring Mac the train would be the slowest and he could easily catch it.

Having hooked trains before proved beneficial for me. I caught the second car behind the engine and as I swung around I looked back to check on McAdams. Mac had missed, but he was waving frantically for me to stay on board. I watched as Mac turned toward Seward for the long eight-mile walk, and the comfort of buying a ticket on the next train.

I climbed on the top of the car and leaned into the wind as the train gained speed. The next car forward was the coal tender, and I figured that would be the warmest place to ride. The light jacket I wore felt as thin as my shirt as I sat down on the back of the coal box and shivered in the chill of the late April evening.

Many coal-burning trains sprayed their coal with water to produce a hotter flame and steam in the firebox. The first spraying caught me by surprise and the fast moving train caused the water to blow back on me. Sitting on the back of the coal tender I had been cold, but now I was soaked with water and shivered until my teeth bit my tongue.

As the train pulled into the railyard in Anchorage, I prepared to jump off before the yard foreman caught me and asked for money I did not have. I struggled to use cold muscles that would not respond. Slowly, I made my way over the side of the coal car and down the iron ladder; I waited until the train had almost stopped for fear I would fall under the wheels.

I jumped and stumbled but did not fall. Grasping my slab of bacon and piece of canvas, I walked across the rail tracks toward town, each step seeming to bring new life to my numb body. Reaching the relative safety of the embankment, I stood gazing at the Chugach Mountains that formed a giant ring around the valley in which Anchorage lay quietly in the early twilight.

The same warm, secure feeling that I had experienced in Ketchikan and again in Seward pervaded me again. I forgot that I was broke, had no place to sleep for the night, and had not eaten since morning.

"I really believe I'm home at last," I said over and over as I stood there drinking deeply of the realization that I had found an emotional sensation that really felt like home.

CHAPTER II

SEARCH FOR SECURITY

Anchorage was the largest city in Alaska in April of 1935, but I found it difficult to describe it as a city. Dirt streets, mostly one-story buildings and an unstable population made it different from the largest city in any other state I had ever been in. Yet, it was this very basic difference that made it Anchorage and part of my Alaska dream.

As I walked along the railyard toward the terminal building, I remembered Grover Cofelt who had joined me and Mac in this Northern adventure. Grover never mentioned money, but he always had enough to pay his way; we traveled together but we never really got acquainted. The man was quiet, soft-spoken, and soon went his own way after we got to Alaska. In Seward, he bought a coach ticket and never entered into our discussion of 'hooking the cars' to get to Anchorage.

As I approached the station, I saw Cofelt coming out of the building. Together, we walked downtown and within an hour he had rented a cabin. After Mac arrived, this cabin served as home for the three of us until jobs dissolved our bonds of common need for each other.

The depression years seemed to foster bonds of helpfulness as men found themselves in the same difficult circumstances. For three men entering into a strange new world so far from the familiar one we had left, there was a particularly strong bond of camaraderie. Each of us was willing to share whatever we possessed. Mac was welcomed into the cabin when the train arrived the next day.

Early that first morning, after having warmed from the train ride and slept eight full hours, I dressed and walked out into the crisp morning air. April nights are usually cold in Anchorage, but the days are warm enough to melt the lingering snow. April is a delightful time of year. The long winter nights finally give way to the lengthening days and winter loses its grip as spring struggles to be born. Southern Alaska, south of the Alaska Range, is usually a few weeks ahead of the Interior in reaching out for summer. To a young emigrant from Idaho, it seemed almost perfect to me. There was just something in the air, something entirely different about the mountains looming large in the early morning darkness—a kinship, a love affair, that continued to grow with each passing year.

I inhaled deeply, and with a sigh of satisfaction, I hurried back to the warmth of our cabin. I discovered that walking briskly was not enough to keep me warm, when the only clothes I owned were my BVDs, a pair of light trousers, a shirt and sport jacket. But the chill was not enough to hinder my enjoyment of this new-found home.

"Since this is going to be my land," I said half aloud, "I'm going to start my life over again. In fact, I'm going to go to church Sunday and prove it."

I had not been religious in most instances. Odd jobs, rough crowds and travelling on the boxing circuit had not been the best ingredients for righteous living, I'm sure.

In high school, I had been the fastest runner in Idaho. I ran the mile in 4:48 in 1922, thirty-three years before the four minute mile was achieved by Roger Bannister. I was an all-around athlete, and made the football team my freshman year in Weiser Intermountain Institute in Weiser, Idaho. I lettered in basketball, football and track each of my four years there.

Boxing was not a school sport at the Institute, but I learned the art well because I enjoyed the competition. During elementary school, I moved often with my family. My father worked on the railroad as a foreman building trestles; when a job was completed we moved to the next town—and school. Each school had its own "bully" and the constant challenge of those early years was the new boy in school. The local bully had to prove his coveted position.

I was fast and scrappy even as a nine year old. I took on every bully and never lost a fight. After high school, this backyard training was put to good use that would serve me throughout life.

Turning semi-professional as a boxer in 1924, I soon realized there was easy money in the ring for a quick, agile fighter. With the decision made, I demanded to be classed as a professional—the pay was better, and I thought perhaps the future, too.

I fought twenty-five professional fights and never lost, though there were two classified as "draws." I am left-handed and few people defend properly against a left-hook.

So this decision to "start life over again" and prove it by going to church was not an outgrowth of a Sunday School dropout. It was a decisive move on my part to answer a deeper longing—a new land seemed to call for a new life.

Alaska presented me with a perfect first Sunday. The sun was warm, prospects of finding work seemed good, the beauty was still breathtaking; I intended to make good my vow and go to church. Putting on the only clothes I possessed, and combing my heavy head of hair until it was slicked down, I put on my light jacket and walked to the first church I could find. Finding a church wasn't difficult; the town was small and the church was large and obvious in its downtown location. As I entered, services had not started so I found a seat and watched others coming into the church. However, as I watched their faces, no one seemed very happy to be in a house of worship, I thought. The solemn, and sometimes sad, faces were immobile as they went through the motions of worship. On cue everyone stood for the benediction, and the slow procession of reaching the front door began. I smiled when it seemed someone was looking in my direction. Outside I lingered for awhile. No one spoke to me, welcomed me, or invited me back. I tried not to make any vows or judgments. I just didn't go back to church again.

After a week in Anchorage, I got a job on a gang surveying homestead sites in the Matanuska Valley for the government colonists coming to Alaska. I had applied for a job as a cook with the Alaska Railroad, but I took the first opportunity for work.

I went downtown to one of the stores and told the owner that I had a job, but I needed a grubstake until payday. I was allowed to buy clothes, a sleeping bag, and anything else a man could need, just on the strength of my word. Alaska was like that then.

After a month on the survey gang, the Alaska Railroad shovel gang boss sent word to me he needed a cook. The pay was better, and the mosquitoes were easier to fight in a kitchen. So I caught the next train for Anchorage where I was hired. Our rail gang then went to Curry, Alaska where I cooked until the Fourth of July.

People seemed to gravitate to town on the Fourth of July. The Railroad recognized the mass exodus and shut down all crews along the line to allow them to celebrate. After the celebration, I was sent with a different crew into the McKinley Park area for the remainder of the summer.

I was head cook for the gang and had the responsibility of ordering the necessary supplies from Anchorage. Things were going well until one week my shipment of supplies arrived with only half the amount of beef I had ordered. When I complained to my boss in Anchorage, who was new on the job, he decided to straighten out the head cook at McKinley on these matters and caught the next train from town. He arrived in the kitchen as I was starting to prepare the evening meal. The argument that followed should not be related in detail, but it ended when I pulled my apron off, threw it in the face of the yelling boss, and said, "I quit—you fix supper for them." My surprised boss then exclaimed, "You can't quit, I don't have another cook but myself." Without looking back, I calmly said, "Then you cook supper." He had to do that for the next two weeks until a new cook could be found.

I caught the next train back to Anchorage and went out on another shovel gang as a laborer in Girdwood, Alaska.

In Girdwood, I decided that if I was to be an Alaskan, I had to kill a bear. There were lots of bears in the area. I had killed game in Idaho and was no stranger to hunting. So I had bought a 30-40 Krag rifle and decided to go alone.

Walking up one of the dry glacial creeks that had ceased to flow with fall approaching, I decided to climb a hill and look over the contryside for bear. Across the valley between the two mountains I saw a black bear feeding on late summer berries. I carefully made my way back to the creek, and walked upstream until I felt sure that I was about even with the bear. At this point, the righthand embankment was steep and about forty feet high. Climbing was slow and difficult. By the time I finally reached the top I was out of breath. And I crawled over the top only to discover that I was less than ten feet from the bear. When the bear heard me he turned and stood on his hind feet. From my belly position on the ground, that bear looked ten feet tall! Without aiming,

I quickly brought the rifle to my shoulder and fired. The bear rolled eighty feet down the backside of the hill and didn't so much as twitch. When I reached him he was very dead. With darkness approaching, and the prospect of a long pack back to camp, the thrill of this hunt came to a rapid conclusion. Later, when I trudged into camp with the skin and a hunk of meat on my back, I felt like a real Alaskan.

A few days after the bear hunt, I was working with the shovel gang along the tracks when a dirt and rock slide gave way just above me. Everything happened so fast that even the agility I had acquired in the boxing ring was of little use in escaping the mass of dirt and rock coming almost straight down the embankment. I jumped, but the slide pinned me against a rail car and burried me waist deep. I felt neither pain nor panic as the rest of the crew came running to dig me out. I soon discovered, however, that my calmness was the result of shock. Before the dirt was cleared, I became acutely aware of a sharp pain in my right leg. They took me to the government hospital in Anchorage to be checked. I remained there for several weeks with a fractured thigh.

By the time I could walk again, the railroad crews were laid off for the winter. I had saved my money, and felt that I could survive the winter, but work was a big part of my life. As long as I can remember, work was a joy and a challenge. Once as a boy in Idaho, my father started a large garden to supplement the family income while he was between jobs. The plan was for my father, Alfred, to work the two-acre plot with help from the boys, particularly me. The garden was well underway when a sawmill called Dad to work. So he turned the garden responsibility over to me; I was only twelve years old. School was a hindrance, but I got up at daybreak each day and worked the garden before school. After school, I often worked until dark. My father was amazed to see the cleanest, finest garden in Idaho on his next visit home.

The only job I ever lost was when I was nine. I had gotten a job pulling weeds for one of the businessmen in town for fifteen cents an hour. I then hired my cousin for ten cents an hour to help me. After a few days, my cousin decided the boss was rich and talked me into "striking" for higher wages. Instead of more money, the boss declared the position vacant and we were out of work. My cousin didn't seem to mind, but after a few days, I went back to the man and asked for my job back—at the same pay. The man hired me with one stipulation—I must not hire that troublemaking cousin again!

With the railroad work closed for the winter, I headed back to Palmer.

27

That young town was growing up as the Matanuska Valley filled with colonists. I heard that homes were being built for the colonists and the town was booming. So I knew that opportunity beckoned.

Arriving in Palmer late in the evening, I began asking folks about work. The civic center was under construction, and sewer and water construction was still in high gear trying to beat the weather clock that would soon shut all work down. I worked at several jobs until the middle of December, when construction work played out.

Jobs were not plentiful in Idaho during December of 1935. I sent money to my brother, Mike, to come to this new land that seemed to not know the depression was anything more than newspaper talk. Mike arrived shortly before Christmas although there would be no work until spring.

There was plenty of homestead land near Palmer, but there were no roads. The Anchorage-Palmer road had the slashing cut, but was not yet a road. The land was new, virgin country; not free, but it didn't cost money. Mike and I decided to file on a 160-acre plot that would be close to the new road when completed.

We had to trudge seven miles on that cold December day in order to reach the land I had in mind. Full packs and new snow are natural enemies to any man on the trail; by mid-afternoon we reached the hillside overlooking a small valley that we felt would be a natural for farming and ranching.

As we stood looking at the breathless beauty of a winter-wonderland and dreamed of the cattle on a thousand hills, we were brought back to reality by the large, gentle flakes of falling snow. Winter is a reality you must not forget on the trail. Night was fast approaching and our only shelter was the trees.

Mike set about clearing an area of snow while I cut small birch saplings to build a lean-to. In an hour we had shelter, crude though it was, and the roaring fire swallowed the falling snowflakes before they blew inside. After supper, we were two tired men who crawled into their sleeping bags and slept soundly with exhausted, aching bodies.

I was awakened by the bright morning sun glistening on six inches of new snow. The fire had lost its battle with the falling flakes; only black ends of burned logs looked at me through the heavy blanket of white. The weather was cold, in spite of the sunshine, and we were anxious to begin building better shelter.

A cabin site was selected after breakfast. The snow was kicked aside and stakes were driven for a 16' x 14' cabin. The first logs were felled as near the site as possible. They were trimmed, cut to length, and laid in place before noon. Both Mike and I were experienced ax-men from lumbering in Idaho and the work went smoothly. We had all of our trees marked, cut, trimmed, and dragged to the site within three days. We were proud of our progress, but on the third day a log rolled the wrong way and pinned my ankle. Although my ankle hurt, I continued to hobble and work for the rest of the afternoon. By morning my ankle was so swollen that I couldn't get my boot on. Unable to walk into town, I could only lay in the lean-to. When the cold became unbearable I hobbled out and built up the fire. After three days, the swelling went down, but the soreness lasted longer.

By the time I was able to walk again, all the logs had been trimmed and lay ready to be used. Other nearby homesteaders came to help and the cabin walls were raised in one day. We were grateful men as we thanked our neighbors for their help. That night was our best night on the homestead.

Mike and I put the roof on our cabin the next day. When we moved into the little house, it seemed like a mansion. Not many mansions, however, have cracks in the walls that you can see through. But any shelter seemed better than the canvas lean-to we'd had the past ten days.

On our first trip in, I had tied a seventy pound cook stove on my packboard and Mike carried most of the foodstuff. The stove was installed in the new cabin and a hot fire seemed to promise a night of relative comfort.

We were awakened from sleep about midnight by a raging wind. Winds in this area can frequently reach eighty miles per hour or more. The cabin was so cold that we climbed up on a shelf we had built near the ceiling to get away from the wind that came through the cracks in our walls. I don't recall that it was much warmer near the ceiling, but I do remember that we were about frozen to death by morning.

We needed to chink the cracks if we were to survive. However, the snow was deep and the moss was frozen hard at this time of year. Yet, something had to be done.

Next morning, I remembered seeing an old Yukon stove in an abandoned cabin we had passed on the trail. Mike said he had noticed some old canvas tarping near the slash cut of the Palmer road. If we could chink the cracks with the canvas and heat with the Yukon stove, perhaps our cabin would be livable. So this is what we set out to do.

I was the first to return to the cabin. I installed the stove and built a hot fire. Then I walked to the door to look for Mike. From the cabin door I could see a mile toward the slash road.

What I saw looked like a giant spider, about a mile down the trail, just inching toward me. It turned out to be Mike with the biggest roll of tarping on his packboard I have ever seen. I think he really wanted to make sure we filled all the cracks. It was late afternoon before Mike finally reached the cabin and we set about thawing the roll of tarping. As soon as the canvas could be cut, we began chinking the north wall which faced the wind. We worked all night cutting, poking, and wedging canvas into every crack and hole we could find in the walls. By morning our cabin was warm, and cozy enough to melt the snow on the floor. Mike shot a moose a few days later, and the brief winter sun seemingly got warmer every day.

One winter in the northern latitudes will make a person aware that after December 22 something begins to happen in nature. This pivotal date marks the time when the sun has reached 23½ degrees south latitude—the north polar region is tilted as far away from the sun as it will go—and the slow journey toward another date with destiny on June 21 has begun. On that date the opposite tilt occurs and creates the longest day of the year for Alaskans. At first, the movement is imperceptable. Only a couple of minutes of sunshine is gained each day at first, but the psychology of winter darkness is whipped. Everything seems upbeat after December 21, and the long starlit hours, often punctuated by the drifting and dancing aurora borealis, are inched aside daily by the longer arching race of the sun toward summer.

I'm sure it was this pleasant transition of nature—as well as running low on supplies—that prompted me and Mike to snowshoe the seven miles into Palmer one early spring day in 1936. Neither of us expected the changes that were set in motion by a chance meeting on the streets of Palmer.

A friend greeted us as we walked into town. The conversation soon got around to jobs and money and the things that men talk about after being half-frozen for months in Alaska's winter darkness. Half-jokingly, the man said, "Well, I hear the Colony Barber Shop is up for grabs and anyone can cut hair as good as what's being done there now."

Since I was eleven years old I had cut my brother's hair, and anyone else willing to submit to twenty minutes in a chair; I had picked up pocket money in school because I would trim hair cheaper than the local barber. After school I had thought about being a barber and even attended a barber college for a while.

"You know, Mike, I just might ought to look into that Barber Shop deal," I said, as we walked down the street.

"Listen, Ted, you never barbered like that before in your life, you can't just start being a barber," Mike tried to reason. I laughed and said, "Well, a man doesn't really know what he can do unless he gives it a whirl. Let's talk to them anyway."

The Barber Shop in question was the government-owned, but privately leased, shop in Palmer for the new colonists. We went to the federal office building and soon located the agent in charge of leasing the shop. The government needed the shop reopened. The former lessee had headed south when the winter got cold, and that spring day almost anyone could have opened the shop with no money down and a promise to pay.

With the brass and determination that often spelled success for me, I opened the doors of the Colony Barber Shop in the spring of 1936 believing full well I could cut hair as well as any barber in the world. If I failed, I would turn the best side of the haircut to the mirror and talk the man into believing it was the best job north of Seattle—which it probably was.

Mike, knowing that there was no changing me once I had decided an issue, found other work. The homestead in the hills that had occupied our winter was never to become ours. It had been just another adventure that seemed to hold a pot-of-gold at the end of a distant rainbow. Somehow that dream was never materialized.

Instant success could not have come at a better time. Business in the Colony Barber Shop was brisk. Strangely enough, the customers came back. The rent was low and the price of a haircut was high; money began to accumulate for me as the operator of Palmer's only Barber Shop. I soon realized that most of the men in the valley were married homesteaders. And if their wives were like most women. They too would pay—to have their hair cut, curled and coiffured; there was not a beauty salon in town.

I went to Anchorage and arranged for a beautician to come to Palmer once a week. I cut the women's hair and the beautician gave them permanents on a thirty percent commission. Again, it was instant money. Sometimes we worked all night with appointments around the clock. It was not unusual to give fifteen to seventeen permanents—with haircuts—before the dog-tired beautician and I wrapped up the weekend and called it a success.

I saved my money. But by December, 1936, even the money didn't seem important enough to keep me in Palmer. Winter was in full swing when I decided to give up the lease and go south.

This time I traveled without going last class. Mike had a good job in the sawmill near Palmer and decided to work until the winter closed it down. Christmas at the family table seemed far more inviting to me than another winter in the hills. Little did I realize that Palmer, the ranch I dreamed about, and the tiny 12′ x 16′ cabin we'd labored desperately to build were about to be left for good.

CHAPTER III

"THE BEST LAID PLANS..."

The daily train from Anchorage to Palmer was the only link the settlers had with that seaport city. As I rode the slow train through the winding passes of the Chugach Mountains, my thoughts turned to my first trip into Anchorage two years before when I had hooked the train outside of Seward. The thrill of the new land, the expectations of new opportunity had borne fruit for me in two short years. I had arrived broke and without clothes except what I had on my back. Now I had money, clothes, and my vacation would be by passenger ship—both ways!

In December 1936, the shipping industry was on strike and the Port of Anchorage lay still and quiet beneath the winter snow as our train pulled into the terminal. I got a hotel room to wait out the strike settlement which seemed imminent—if street opinions were worth anything.

I was pleasantly surprised that first evening in the hotel lobby when I saw the familiar face of Ted "Mac" McAdams coming toward me. He was the same McAdams that had started this northern adventure two years before, with the casual comment in the Idaho sheep camp where I was working, when he said simply, "Let's go to Alaska!"

McAdams had brought the mail to me in a sheep camp where I had been for over a month. Mac had been a rancher, but the depression had ruined him. He had everything he owned in the old pickup truck he was driving that day. As we sat talking, I read the letter from Ethel Sneed in Ketchikan. The age of mining machinery was coming to Alaska and her glowing description of the impending boom had sounded good to McAdams.

I thought for a moment that day, then said to him, "But what will you do about your ranch?"

"Everything I own is right there in that truck, I'm ready to go if you say so," he replied.

"Well, I tell you what, you take me to town so I can draw my wages and we'll go," I concluded.

We shared those first experiences again as we dined in the hotel coffee shop. McAdams had been cooking for the railroad most of the two years since we arrived, but had been layed off when work slowed for the winter.

As we sat talking about what had happened since our meager start in Idaho, a third man walked to our table. He smelled of liqour and his glazed eyes seemingly reflected the quantity of his consumption, but he walked straight and talked coherently. I knew him as a newspaper printer and introduced him to McAdams as Alaska Morgan.

"Alaska Morgan," Mac chuckled, "Nobody is named Alaska in Alaska." Without a smile, the new friend looked him squarely in the eye and said simply, "I am." Mac never questioned his name again.

"Listen, McRoberts, I've got a deal you will be interested in," Morgan began, ignoring McAdams after the brief encounter.

"Not interested! I'm going home for Christmas, and if this strike doesn't end I am going to buy a partnership in a fishing boat and make some big money this year down on the Kenai."

"Now, Mac, just hold on till you hear me out," he said. "There is a new gold rush starting on Ophir creek and Takotna supplies that whole area. They don't have an active newspaper, but there is one where we can buy real cheap...and you know I'm a good newspaper man.

"Well, if it's such a good deal, why don't you just go buy it without me?" I said.

"The truth of the matter is, I'm a little short on funds at the moment, though it is only temporary," Morgan confided.

We waited ten days in Anchorage before weather permitted us to fly to Takotna on the Star Airlines, forerunner of Alaska Airlines. On January 10, 1937 the skies were clear in Anchorage. The pilot decided to take our group over the mountains and into the Kuskokwim flats. The owner of Star Airlines allegedly told him to leave us on some isolated lake if he had to, but just to get us on our way and out of his hair.

The weather remained good as we turned and banked through mountain passes, but as we neared the flats we saw dark clouds forming a solid wall ahead of us. The pilot decided to go around the storm. Dropping altitude as ice began to form on the wings, the ceiling lowered until we were skimming over the river bed with mountains reaching into the dark mist on each side. Soon the ice became so heavy on the wings that the pilot decided to set the plane down on the river ice. The plane glided smoothly to a stop and everyone jumped out. The snow that held the plane's weight on skiis was a different matter on foot. We sank waist deep in soft, wet snow!

Only one person on board had snowshoes. He broke trail to the bank while the other four of us, Ted McAdams, Alaska Morgan, the pilot, and myself, wallowed our way in fresh snow to the shelter of trees on the bank.

I carried the only hand axe, so I began cutting poles to place under the plane's skiis, to keep them from freezing solid in the snow.

Soaking wet from our ordeal, we needed a fire. The fellow with snowshoes started up the river to locate a cabin we saw just before landing. The other men got busy looking for dead wood while I began felling trees to burn. Deep snow covered most of the dead wood, and the damp, green trees would not burn well. Finally, we got a small fire started and began eating emergency rations from the plane.

With the coming darkness the wind ceased and the stars were bright in the sky. We went back to the plane for our sleeping gear. The calmness of the night was deceptive; we decided to bed down under the wing of the plane. Everyone was wet and cold as we huddled together, shivering for what seemed hours before sleep finally came.

We soon discovered nature was not finished tormenting us. A warm chinook (a south wind that usually brings warm air into the interior) blew up the Kuskokwim that night bringing rain to the frozen interior. Sheltered underneath the wing, we did not awaken at first. But soon the wind began blowing forcefully and we pulled the bedding over our heads. Finally, the rain penetrated the bedding on the side where I lay. So in the drowziness of sleep, I pulled the edge of the padding up to form a dam to keep the water out. The dam didn't take long to break, and we all came alive. We were *really* wet now.

We had anchored our plane to the river ice by chopping holes and freezing tie-down ropes into the ice immediately after landing. Even with the thirty knot wind, the plane seemed the best protection to us. We spent the rest of the night inside the plane, huddled and cramped like a bunch of wet rats.

The wind continued to increase in velocity. And at dawn we abandoned the plane for fear it would be flipped by the wind.

A piece of canvas from the equipment in the plane made a good windbreak after we reached the timber. We managed to start a fire with dead wood and this warmed our dampened spirits after a wet, miserable night.

The thought of eating seemed to occur to everyone at once. Two of us were cooks so we put on a sourdough standby—a pot of beans.

Although the storm died down by mid-morning, the mercury also began to drop. Our fire generated enough heat to cook beans, but not enough to dry our wet bedding and clothing. If the temperature continued dropping, the possibility of us freezing to death was no longer a joke.

We decided to try to break the plane loose and taxi down the river to the cabin we had seen, and that our fifth member had snowshoed to. About this time one of the boys spied our fifth member returning. He was carrying several pair of extra snowshoes.

"The cabin up there belongs to a native man I know," he called out as he approached. "Although they are short of groceries and the menfolk have gone for supplies, his wife said we were welcome to stay there for shelter until the weather breaks."

Our makeshift camp came apart much faster than it had been constructed. The gear and hot pot of beans were loaded into the plane. Then, with us chopping and shoveling away the snow and ice, winter grudgingly released its grip on the Star Airlines flight that was overdue in Takotna. The pilot taxied close to the bank, hoping that the overrun ice was frozen beneath the blanket of wind-swept snow. We led the way on showshoes to pack a trail for the plane and to test the ice as best we could.

When we arrived at the cabin, we again cut poles to place under the

36

skiis. Some heavy logs were lashed to the plane—in case the wind returned.

Satisfied that the plane was secured, we grabbed the partially cooked pot of beans and emergency rations, and hurried to the cabin. The native family moved into the kitchen of their two-room log cabin, giving the front room to us. Within minutes our wet clothes were hanging all around the stove, on which sat the pot of boiling beans. We then lounged in our drying BVD's while children kept peeking through the door at the strange spectacle. I remember someone remarking that it seemed especially good just to be alive. But unresponsive yawns were our only response as we dropped off to sleep.

Mrs. Gregory loaned us some skins to supplement what dry bedding we had salvaged from the plane. The haphazard arrangement on the tiny cabin floor in no way deterred our dreams of a better tomorrow.

The temperature continued dropping during the night. By morning, the snow had frozen enough to enable our plane to take off with a full load; we left our extra rations with Mrs. Gregory to express our gratitude. The little plane raced over the frozen snow and climbed into the sky. Within twenty minutes Takotna was below us and the pilot skillfully slid the plane to a stop on river ice. We were in Takotna at last.

CHAPTER IV

THE TRIALS AND TRIUMPHS IN TAKOTNA

The three men standing outside the door when Mr. E.A. Rask answered our knock that dreary January day did not look like business men—and less like men with money. Mr. Rask owned "The Kusko Times," a good sounding name of a disjointed newspaper. McAdams warmed himself by the potbellied stove while Alaska Morgan and I questioned Rask about the building and equipment of *The Kusko Times*.

The paper had been in production since 1922, but a well-known roadhouse proprietor in McGrath, a man named Hoskins, had acquired the plant from Mr. Rask with the idea of moving the paper from Takotna to McGrath. Hoskins put the equipment on his sledges and pulled it overland by caterpillar to McGrath—18 miles from Takotna—via an old sled road. The sled road was used in winter to freight supplies from McGrath.

The paper had been inoperative for several years when it was purchased by Hoskins. The old Army printing press and other equipment, with the exception of the linotype machine, were loaded up, and the proud purchaser started over the trail to McGrath. Snow had been falling heavily for days; it would be smart not to overload the sledges, Hoskins told some friends. But the excessive weight of type and parts was deceptive. Six feet of new snow was on the ground, and the snow was sticky and wet. When the caterpillar became mired about three miles from town, the new owner simply unhooked his sleighs and left them to the elements.

As Mr. Rask finished telling the story of scattered newspaper equipment, he ended by saying, "Besides, you will have to see Mr. Hoskins to make the necessary arrangements for the purchase." At that moment, neither Morgan nor I was sure it was worth the effort to find Hoskins. But Rask continued by saying, "In the meantime, you can bunk in the back of *The Kusko Times* building—pending final approval of the purchase, of course." Needing a place to stay, we accepted the offer. A few days later I paid $500 and became owner of the scattered press. I paid another $500 for the little log building to put it in.

I found a stack of books and manuals on the linotype and began to tear the rusty, inoperative machine apart. The oil lamp burned into the night as part by part and page by page I dismantled the equipment I had never seen before. I cleaned each part and carefully laid them in order; several parts were broken. Takotna was the service center for the gold fields. I figured they must have a machinist. I took the broken parts and began to inquir if anyone in town could make me new ones. My questions soon led to a machinist who turned out to be a genius at improvising almost anything. After the parts were made the tedious process of reconstruction began; part by part, page by page I reassembled the equipment that now seemed almost a part of me.

When the last bolt was in place, I stood back and admired my job, then realized I couldn't test it to see if it worked. I had never seen a linotype before and didn't know for sure what it was supposed to do. That was a job for Morgan.

"Hey, Morgan, I've got this thing fixed, come check it out," I called.

Morgan stood looking at the clean, almost sparkling machine and said, "Mac, I don't even believe what I see, but it probably won't work."

The gasoline engine which powered the press and linotype was given a quick check. To our amazement, the engine started the first time we cranked it over. While Morgan sat down and began punching keys on the linotype with far more skepticism than conviction, the clanging and banging of the engine drowned out my yells of jubilation. It worked perfectly!

Then we hired a freighter in Takotna to rescue the rest of our stranded newspaper. With dog teams, he and I travelled to a pile of snow blocking the trail to McGrath. Underneath the snow we found the old Army press, gasoline engines, type, parts and the rest of the missing newspaper. Trip by trip the dogs pulled the missing parts back to the log house of *The Kusko Times*. Morgan directed the placement of the equipment in the newspaper building and *The Kusko Times* was reborn. In less than three weeks, we had purchased the paper and gotten the first edition into the hands of the people. The date was Saturday, February 5, 1937.

Alaska Morgan was a newspaper man. Mechanically, Morgan couldn't build a fire, but boy, that man could put out a newspaper, so we agreed that I'd go drum up business and he would meet the deadline.

Starting in Takotna, I knocked on almost every door within a radius of 250 miles during the next few months. I used snowshoes, dog teams, and when the river thawed I used a riverboat; everyone became a prospect for our tiny paper.

The people really wanted to see that paper go. They didn't get much news and it was a real service to them. I can't remember anyone turning me down for an ad or subscription.

The Kusko Times reached people in the Bristol Bay area, along the coast, and in most of the Camps along rivers of western Alaska. I became known to whites and natives alike. I tried to be friendly, honest and as personable as possible—all of this later made me a Marshal the people trusted.

One of the first news stories I decided to write brought me into contact with a person who changed my life.

The news isn't difficult to narrow in a town the size of Takotna; a story on the local school seemed a logical choice to me. I went to the little one-room school in the early darkness of winter, after the children had gone. The only teacher lived in the building and I began to bang on the front door of the school. Eventually, I heard footsteps and the door opened. An attractive, well-kept lady, younger than me, invited me in. We went to a small lighted room in the back of the school, unbelievably small for living quarters, and I explained to her that I wanted to do a story for the newspaper. I tried to ask questions but my mind kept wondering, first at the difficult living conditions for such an attractive woman, and secondly, about the woman herself. Little did I know the part she would play in my life from that moment on.

News is news wherever you find it. Local news was no problem. Sometimes it was just "word of mouth", but I developed a knack for

41

sifting out the factual content in local news. Getting national and international news was more difficult. I purchased a short-wave radio and listened each night to the news from New York and San Francisco—or any other station that happened to come in clearly. I would jot down the events as best I could as the crackling and fading distant voices filtered through the long wire antenna into my snow-covered hut in an area unknown to most of the outside world. The aurora borealis became a nemesis to me as a Takotna newsman. When the dancing lights played in the arctic sky, H.V. Katenborn spoke only half his words on the late, late news. To hear the seven o'clock news from New York meant I had to tune in at three a.m. Takotna time. I would jot down what I was able to understand, then fill in the missing words as best I could. No one ever mentioned the difference—even if sports events didn't always give both scores. World events moved more slowly in those years—what was missed one night usually could be filled in the next.

The Kusko Times was delivered by mail to most of the mining camps. Takotna had a post office and most of the camps got weekly mail, sometimes by boat, sometimes by plane, or backpack. In the winter, dog teams made regular runs to the camps with the mail; *The Kusko Times* brought a glimpse of neighbors, the latest Roosevelt attempt to break the depression, and even the sabre rattling of the goose-stepping German youth under Hitler, as the world moved closer to a war that would change Takotna as much as it changed the world.

In the spring of 1938, I sold my share of the *Times* to my partner, Alaska Morgan. Morgan eventually defaulted on payment and I later sold the equipment to Jack Burger. Jack wanted it shipped to Kodiak where he intended to set up the paper and resell it. I crated the entire press and shipped it to McGrath via the Takotna River, then by stern-wheeler to Bethel where a steamer took it to Kodiak. Burger never paid any of the freight or purchase price. The press that had been resurrected from its snow-covered grave on the McGrath trail, died on the docks of Kodiak. I never heard from the equipment again, and each time I met Burger the answer was always the same, "You know, Ted, I'll pay you as soon as I can, but right now I'm a little short on funds." Burger had been like many miners in those days. He struck gold on one claim and made $44,000 in one season. It seemed so good he and his partner put every cent into heavy equipment to work the strike. Two days after beginning operation with the new equipment, the vein petered out. Jack enjoyed the women and liquor more than a newspaper and it just never worked out.

The Kusko Times made good money, but I was a physical man who craved activity. When Alaska Morgan offered to buy the paper it seemed like a God-send to me. Ted McAdams, my former partner who seemed to always offer a new adventure, had been trying to get me to go into partnership as a freighter. His plan was to build a boat and barge and compete for the summer freight traffic from McGrath to Takotna.

After selling the paper in the Spring of 1938, I decided to try this new partnership. We built the first tunnel-drive riverboat in the area and ordered a 40 horse marine engine for it. The barge was built to carry five tons and we planned to push it with the boat. The big sternwheelers couldn't navigate the Takotna river and mining activity was picking up along Ophir creek; freight prospects were excellent.

The Takotna river had many sandbars, shallows and rapids in the 65 miles from Takotna to McGrath. The downstream trip was usually a pleasant, restful trip. But the return trip, with a full load, would take us from 24 to 36 hours. Most of our time was spent pushing and pulling, jumping into the cold water or heaving on a tow rope tied to the barge—never resting—once we started the return trip.

We never changed clothes once we started; Old-timers said if we would never change clothes while wet we would never catch cold. We never changed clothes and we never caught cold, so I guess they were right.

After several trips between McGrath and Takotna, my penchant for something different began to change my mind. The water seemed colder each time I jumped in, but the money in freight hauling was good. So I thought, why not truck it from Takotna to Ophir? At least I wouldn't have to jump in the river everytime the truck stalled!

I ordered a truck from Seattle in late summer, barely making the last boat into McGrath before freeze-up. We loaded it on the barge and hauled my prized possession to Takotna. Two other trucks were working the haul to Ophir creek. But with the connections I had made in the newspaper business, and after a successful summer of freight hauling, my business remained good. When warm weather activity on the river ceased, only that freight which had to be moved was hauled over the sled road from McGrath. So we dry-docked our operation until spring.

I became manager of the N.C. Co. store in Takotna for the winter and maintained contacts which provided our first freight contract after breakup the following spring. This contract enabled me to buy a second truck before operations ceased in late September. The trucks were my operation and Mac and I remained partners in the river freight, too.

Winter came early to the Kuskokwim delta rivers in the fall of 1939. Captain Hootnanny Johnson, of the sternwheeler *Alaskan*, knew the Kuskokwim as well as any man alive. But even he was taken by surprise on his last run to McGrath. The ice flows began to thicken and shallows along the bank turned white and became still as his riverboat crept upstream. A decision had to be made: make it to McGrath and risk being frozen in for the winter, or unload the cargo on the bank and head back downstream.

"Heave to, take a sounding, we're going to put this stuff on the bank up ahead," is the way Hootnanny later told the story. Ice was hitting the hull with jarring force then grinding along the side of the wooden flat-bottom. The water was deep where the current cut into the bank and the decaying cliffs were only a few feet above the water.

"Looks like a ready-made dock just for us," Johnson said as he continued giving orders to dock *The Alaskan*. Work began quickly as they tied along the bank; they rolled more than two hundred barrels of oil and gasoline onto the frozen bank.

Without waiting for the light of a new day, Hootnanny Johnson eased his giant sternwheeler back into the current and toward the safety of more open water.

The miners didn't mind the delay of extra fuel when winter work was slow, but with the coming of summer, they needed fuel badly or work would stop. By now, my name was synonymous with moving freight when freight needed moving; I was contracted to get the fuel from the banks of the Kuskokwim to Ophir creek.

I was to barge those barrels up to Takotna and then truck it to the miners. I could carry about 20 drums on the barge; it was an easy run to Takotna except for one rapids that almost cost me my life.

School was out for the summer, and I had made sure that my friendship with the attractive schoolteacher continued. Her name was Ethyl Peasgood and our friendship was mutual. As I prepared to make another run down river, Ethyl appeared on the dock. The day was warm and the sky clear; my invitation to go along seemed to be the best thing that had happened to her that day I guess, for she climbed aboard.

Any single woman teaching in a village school in Alaska in the late 1930's was self-reliant; Ethyl was especially capable. She could handle a dog team, outboard motor, or chop wood with equal ease. This talent probably saved my life on this last run.

The last twenty drums were loaded and we began the slow trip back to Takotna. I had placed an extra engine on the barge and Ethyl was running the motor on the boat. As we approached the rapids, Mac jumped ashore with a tow rope and I climbed onto the barge with a pike pole to help push the load through the current. With the pole on the lower side of the barge, I would push and Mac would pull. The motors were barely able to hold the distance gained with each effort.

The current caught the barge and swung it around against the pike pole, throwing me off balance. The pole went under the barge and I was flipped overboard on the downstream side. As I fell, I grabbed the gunwale with one hand, but the barge was running on top of me. A short distance below us, at the bottom of the rapids, a huge boulder protruded from the foaming water. The barge was on a collision course with the rock and the motors were helpless. Ethyl left the motor and ran to the barge, grabbing me by my collar she began pulling me on board. I strained every muscle in my arms as the two of us worked to overcome the pushing current. Just as I rolled onto the barge, we hit the rock broadside, almost exactly on the spot were I had been struggling for my life. The barge didn't break; a tree stump had lodged on the rock and broke the impact. The barge lodged on the rock and swung toward the bank until it was wedged tightly; none felt like moving it after the near disaster. McAdams tied the barge rope securely on the bank, we unhooked the boat from the barge and the three of us headed back for Takotna. After the excitement had passed, Ethyl jokingly said, "O.K. Ted, that's one you owe me." In two years I would pay that debt in full.

CHAPTER V

SURVIVAL

The old prospector, Charlie Goebel who claimed to be the black sheep of the Budweiser beer family, sat with his feet propped on the woodbox behind the Yukon stove in my Takotna cabin. Outside, the wind was blowing hard enough to make the chimney produce the deep-throated roar of a distant freight train. The mercury had dropped twenty degrees in the past hour. Bill Pruit was seated opposite the old-timer casually carving tiny wood chips from a piece of birch. I put a container of snow on the stove to melt for coffee water as Goebel continued his story.

"Been up that creek a hunnert times or more and never found anything, but this time it was different. Don't know how much, cause it turned cold fore I did much scratchin, but there's gold in that creek. I got color everytime I dipped my pan, and boys I've been scratchin' this country long enough to know *that* much color's got to come from somewhere."

The old prospector was referring to O.K. creek, about 30 miles up the Takotna river behind Joaquin mountain. The distance there was half as far going straight across, but going straight across most anywhere in the arctic can be painfully difficult.

47

All summer long Pruitt and I talked and dreamed of the big lode just waiting for us back of Joaquin mountain. Money was coming in fast, and we felt financial independence. Why not do what we really want to do? we asked each other almost everyday of the warm summer.

By the first of September, we had convinced each other that the thing to do would be to check out that creek before freeze-up came. All contracts had been fulfilled; no freight was waiting in McGrath; there couldn't be a better time.

Early the next morning we were loading the freight boat before daylight and were ready to head up river in search of our El Dorado before the sun melted the frost on the other boats nearby. The 30-mile ride was slow. The winding river and new water demanded all our attention to miss the logs and rocks just under the surface. By noon, we were at the landing; now we had only to backpack over a high mountain to drop us about where the old prospector said he found gold. As it turned out, the backside of the mountain was as far away as sundown, and the steep climb made us willing to camp for the night on the crest of the mountain. To make travelling easier, we carried only one large down-filled, two-man sleeping bag. The night was cold, and we were sure that it was because we were high on the mountain, exposed to the wind. An unheeded warning can spell disaster in the arctic, but all the gold in the world seemed to be in that creek at the bottom of the mountain. We ignored the falling temperature.

The first pan of gravel produced good color, and the excitement of staking claims hid reality from us. A gambler's spirit quickly took control of us. We were new prospectors and acted the parts. By noon, when hunger prompted us to make tea and eat a handful of raisins, I realized it was turning colder fast. Pruitt insisted on staking just a few more claims; as we worked, a north wind began to blow. Both of us realized similtaneously that we needed to get back to the boat and down river quickly; ice had already started to form on the creek we were working.

We cached our food and equipment, taking only one packboard and our two-man sleeping bag. Pushing our endurance to the point of exhaustion, we reached the top of Joaquin mountain in record time.

The sun was low in the western sky as we topped the mountain that brought the Takotna river into view; our hearts stopped still! As far as we could see in both directions, the river was iced white. It looked like it was flowing, but we were still miles from the boat we had beached the day before. Half running, half falling, we covered the two miles

School picture taken about 1911. Stars on flag indicate it was before Arizona and New Mexico were admitted to the Union in 1912. Ted McRoberts is second from left, front row, and Ethyl Sneed, whose letter lured Ted and McAdams to Alaska is on the bottom row, right end.

Members of the 1921-22 high school class in Animal Husbandry at Montour, Idaho included Ted McRoberts, third from left.

High School graduation photo of Ted upon completion of Weiser Mountain Institute in Montour, Idaho.

Always an avid bird hunter, Ted McRoberts at age fifteen had become an excellent shot. Part of double-barrelled 20-gauge shows in this photograph taken in 1918.

Ted, left, and hunting partner pause on their way up a mountain to hunt goat.

Goat hunting makes hungry hunters. Ted, left, and a friend take timeout for lunch. Ted owned a .30-40 Krag during this period of his life and hunted much of the time with it.

Ted and brother Mike with their first load of gear for the Palmer homestead. Note carefully the size of the pack load on Ted's back.

Makeshift lean-to shelter at homestead site offered protection from the coming winter, but even with a stove inside it could not offer protection for long. The first snowfall of the year is shown here.

Two brothers from a nearby homestead offered to help the McRoberts brothers erect a cabin before winter became too harsh. Homer Hays and his brother are shown with Ted pulling a log to the cabin.

Ted poses for a first picture with the new homestead cabin. Note the giant cracks between the logs needing chinking. The logs fit tighter near the top providing the shelter from the wind when they first moved in.

Always a lover of animals, Ted holds one of his young sled dog puppies outside the Kusko Times building in Takotna. Notice a copy of the newspaper in his hip pocket. The paper succeeded as much from his relentless contact with the gold camps and people in the news as any other thing.

The caterpillar tractor brought overland from the Flat area to Bethel which almost cost Ted far more than the equipment was worth.

Sunday afternoon walks provided much of the leisure activity in Takotna for young adults. Ted and Ethyl Peasgood make a striking couple in their furs.

The hard life of early mining in Alaska is depicted in this scene of Ted and Mike's tent which provide them living quarters all winter.

Always an avid gardner, Ted's garden plot in Takotna was ample enough for other families to use also. Other buldings in the

Ted's cabin in Takotna from the front gives a much better impression of its sturdy log construction. Heated by wood only, it was not difficult to keep warm with plenty of logs available.

Ted's first adventure into hardrock mining was here along O.K. creek. They frequently had to thaw the ground before their drilling was effective. This scene looks toward the head of the drainage.

Ted, holding gold pan, and a hired hand as they work drilling equipment at the O.K. Creek mine. The winter's work produced hardly enough gold to pay expenses, though others along the creek often hit big pay dirt.

The building of the cabin at Sterling Landing for Ted's freighting business from the Kuskokwim River to Takotna. The Kuskokwim River can be seen in the background. Ted is standing on the walls of the cabin. c. 1941.

Sterling cabin finished at last.

The McRoberts family during one of Dads visits to the gold fields of Western Alaska. From left to right, Mike, father Alfred,

down the mountain, with each step further confirming our deepest fears of freeze-up; another mile to the river and all our fears were totally confirmed.

Exhausted, we sat down on the gunwale of our boat and looked at the heavy ice moving slowly downriver. Too tired and too desperate for logic, we launched the boat and made our way into the middle of the river; the motor was almost useless, but gradually we moved. Five minutes, ten minutes, a half hour passed—then we stopped dead still—frozen in the middle of a river, without food or much shelter, and the ice much too rotten to support a man's weight.

"What do we do now?" Pruitt asked blankly, without expecting an answer.

"Looks to me like the only thing left to do is pray," I said in all seriousness. The silence of the stilled ice seemed to bring death closer to reality than either of us had ever experienced before in difficult places. We prayed!

That was one time I really got down and prayed. It must have appeared strange to see a small wooden boat frozen in the earliest freeze-up on record in Alaska with two men kneeling in prayer. While we were praying, we felt the boat move a little and both of us looked up at the same time. The ice began to part in a swath about 10-feet wide in front of the boat and angled downstream toward the bank of the river. We started the motor and headed for the bank through the clear channel of open water. Without looking back we jumped out and dragged the boat upon the bank, then Pruitt said, "Look!" pointing toward the river. The channel of clear water had disappeared.

That night we slept in the boat. The river ice had begun to move again and the loud noise of the grinding and roar of running ice lifted our hopes that by morning we would be able to make it home.

Early the next morning, I awoke first and lay still in the warmth of the sleeping bag. Something wasn't right. Then I realized all I could hear was silence, the sickening silence of a frozen world that has its victim trapped. During the night, the river had stopped moving and the surface was packed tightly with large chunks of ice.

We got up and rolled up our sleeping bag. The situation was serious; all the food and supplies had been left in the cache on O.K. creek. Had the river not been frozen we could have made it back to Takotna in two hours running with the current.

I made it a habit never to go into the wilderness of Alaska without tea. I could go without food for long periods of time, even days, if I had the strength of warm tea to lift my spirits. I built a fire, and made a tin can full of tea. We knew the boat was stuck there for the winter. After tea, we dragged the boat to higher ground and tied it securely to a tree, just in case spring runoff should produce high water nine months later. I climbed a tree and hung the motor higher than any snowfall or spring runoff. Pruitt had the sleeping bag on his back as we started the long, arduous walk out of the frozen country. We had not travelled a tenth of the 40 land-miles home when snow began to fall in large, gentle flakes; soon six inches blanketed the area.

Between each row of hills lay tundra flats that had not frozen hard enough to support a man's weight. Sometimes one of us, other times both of us would break through and get our feet wet up to our knees. Then began a race with time to get a fire going and dry out before frostbite occurred.

We always carried extra socks in our pockets, if not in our packs, for such emergencies. We reasoned that unless our feet were cared for properly we were at the mercy of the unforgiving cold. While we dried our socks and boots, we would make a tin can of tea and eat frozen blueberries—sour, frozen blueberries and tea for three days of walking from daylight until dark!

Mid-afternoon of the third day we arrived at the rapids of the Takotna river about a mile above the village. We could see the outline of the buildings, piled high with the new-fallen snow. Smoke curled lazily upward in the cold September air, and for a brief moment of jubilance we slapped each other on the back and danced around. Then the reality of the situation came to us—we were on the opposite side of the river! The river ice would not yet support our weight; the swift-moving rapids had not frozen.

I knew the river and I knew those rapids, they were shallow enough to wade but with the flowing ice and swift water we hesitated.

Below the mouth of the rapids the river ice was solid on the surface. We could see the huge hunks of ice as they reached the bottom of the rapids and were rolled under the frozen surface of the river.

Pruitt was the first to speak, "We might wade that, Ted, but if a fellow slipped he'd roll under that ice the very same way those chunks are doing."

"I think we can wade here if we get a pole to help us stand up," I said. "I'll go first and when I'm across then you come. That's a good 200-feet wide so don't start until I make it—that way one of us can tell the folks what happened to the other one."

"Don't joke," Pruitt cautioned, "the water would be difficult enough if you didn't run the chance of getting knocked down by that ice."

I waded slowly into the rushing water. After ten steps I could no longer feel my feet and legs, numbed from the icy water. About 20-feet from the bank, I glanced back and Pruitt was starting across. Hip deep in water and off balance from looking over my shoulder, I was struck on the side by a large ice flow. Pruitt saw me fall and dashed the few steps out of the water and downstream as fast as he could run. Grabbing a long, dead limb that had drifted onto the bar, he waited for me as I tumbled and bobbed along until I got within his reach. Fortunately, it had been my turn to carry the sleeping bag which served now to buoy me to the top of the swirling water.

I came up and opened my eyes just in time to see that long limb Pruitt had stretched toward me. I grabbed it and held on, and the current swung me over toward the bank until I could get to my feet. We were just above the river ice when Pruitt reached me. I'm sure Pruitt saved my life that day. I surely would have gone under that ice at the bottom of the rapids.

The north wind never felt so cold. I began to shake so hard I could barely move as we started down the beach to a pile of driftwood. We had to get a fire going as fast as possible. Pruitt was well ahead of me as he crossed a small stream that emptied into the river. The little eddy formed by the backwater was about six feet wide and offered some shelter from the wind. When we got in behind the willow growth we found a boat. Pruitt let out a rebel yell that could have been heard in Takotna had anyone been listening. We knew there was a trapper's log cabin on the opposite bank, if we could get there it would be no problem to warm.

Racing against a freezing clock, we dragged the small boat to the top of the rapids. The open water was less than 100 yards from the head to the foot of the rapids; without oars we would have to pole the 200 feet to the opposite bank. If we were not able to do that, both of us would be stuck in the river ice again. Already my clothes had frozen until I could barely walk. Dodging rocks, banging into heavy ice flows, pushing on the poles in desperation, we beached the boat directly below the cabin.

Trapper cabins were never locked and anyone in need was welcomed to their use. Inside we found fuel: shavings and plenty of dry wood. The Yukon stove, deceptive by its size, puts out as much heat per stick of wood as any method ever devised. The 8' x 10' cabin warmed fast, but I had to thaw the frozen clothing before I could pull it off to dry. As I huddled over the stove, Pruitt began to rummage for something to eat—anything except frozen, sour blueberries.

"Here, I've saved you some of the Grape-Nuts, you want some?" he said.

"Sure. . .and I'll have mine without fruit, please," I said as I reached for the water to pour on the sweetened cereal Pruitt had poured for me.

Gold fever has a way of never letting go of its victims. For a time it will seem to be arrested, but the sight of a nugget, the story of a strike, or just sitting by a stove in a warm cabin thinking what might have been can cause a return of the fever once it's caught. Malaria is much easier to shake than gold fever.

The early winter of 1939, which had caused Hootnanny Johnson to off-load his cargo and make a dash for open water with his sternwheeler, was the same early winter that caught Pruitt and me on O.K. creek. All the rivers of northern Alaska froze early, including the Yukon and Kuskokwim. Freight traffic was at a standstill; I became restless to go back into the area of O.K. creek and stake more claims.

Few men could travel farther on as little food as I could in those days. As I packed my gear to walk the 17 miles over the mountain to O.K. creek, I mixed a little flour, baking soda and shortening together; I could melt a little snow for water and this would make dough. Wrap the dough on a stick and put it next to a fire and it would make bread. I put in some bacon, several handfuls of rice and, of course, my tea. I never went into the woods without an ax and this trip I included a sleeping bag.

I knew about an old trail that led into the creek over Joaquin mountain and I didn't figure we had enough snow to pack snowshoes for just a few days. The trail circled around the mountain, over which we had climbed when the ill-fated boat trip had left us frozen in six weeks earlier, and came into O.K. creek near the head. On the side of the mountain, near the trail, there was an old prospector's cabin. The roof had fallen in, except one corner which provided me the shelter I needed after the 17-mile hike.

As if an angry god would drive us away from O.K. creek, the next morning a blizzard was blowing in all its fury. Snow was falling in a horizontal fashion as I made a small fire in the shelter of the old cabin. Breakfast finished, I rolled my gear and stashed it in the corner that had been my home for the night. Putting a bag of tea in my pocket, I picked up my ax and began to work my way down the creek staking claims.

During the brief daylight hours, I worked hard to stake claims in blowing snow. As night drew near, I noticed another log cabin on the bank of the creek and decided to spend the night in it. The old cabin had not been used for years, but a few supplies were still on hand. An old tin stove, partially rusted out, heated the cabin warm very quickly. I found another can which provided what had been sugar before it melted into a solid cake, brown and hard. Melting snow, I made tea and ate the hard sugar; then I stoked the fire, lay down next to the stove and slept the whole night through without waking.

The next morning the weather had not improved. Twenty-four hours of blizzard had made it difficult to work, but I staked two more claims and decided to return to my gear and go home.

With my mind off my work, I noticed the pain developing in my eyes. They watered and hurt as I worked my way back up the creek. The swirling snow had filtered into my sheltered corner, but I brushed most of it aside and built a little fire. I mixed some dough and wrapped it on a stick to bake. Using a can for a kettle, I boiled the last of my rice. After supper I crawled into my sleeping bag; surely a good night's sleep would ease the increasing pain in my eyes.

The morning of the third day was no different, with one exception. That morning when I awoke, I was blind! My eyes were swollen shut from the snow blindness. All day the relentless storm raged. The snow became heavier and the wind drifted the stinging flakes into the opening of my sleeping bag. I crawled from my sleeping bag and felt on the ground until I found enough sticks to start a fire. More by instinct than by sight, I carefully sheltered the precious matches from the wind. One, two, three matches—it had to light this time, the fourth match. I felt the warmth increase as the shavings began to catch.

Soon I could open my eyes ever so lightly, but the pain was almost unbearable—besides I could see only outlines, not details. The smoke from the fire irritated my eyes even more. Throughout the day I busied myself by carefully making my way to a dead tree and breaking limbs for wood, then glimpsing to be sure of my direction, I would slowly make my way back to the shelter of the fallen roof and the cabin corner. At night, the wood from the caved-in roof would furnish fuel close at hand.

The morning of the fourth day was better. The storm had let up. I knew survival depended on getting home soon. Squinting through blurred vision, I shouldered my pack and began the arduous climb back over the mountain trail. Giant granite boulders littered the mountain; no problem for men with eyes, but to a snow-blinded victim they became deadly obstacles. Slipping in between two boulders, I wrenched my leg. The pain was so excruciating I thought I had broken it. My foot was pinned for what seemed hours before I could free it. After the pain eased, I determined only a small cut. No broken bones, thank God for that, I thought. But the pain was much greater than the cut. I began to feel cheated and angry. When I realized what I felt, it frightened me. I thought I was getting delirious, and I knew it would be fatal to become disoriented.

After crossing the mountain, the rest would be easy—through a heavy stand of spruce, across a swampy area, over the flats and then home. Familiar with the area, my confidence began to rise. I had never doubted my ability to get home, it just seemed easier now.

The heavy snow had buried the swamp where warm springs seeped and the ice wasn't frozen hard underneath. I heard the cracking sound too late and then felt the water on both feet. Still blind, the feel of water startled me and I fell in my effort to avoid the breakthrough. My feet and clothes were wet, and the mercury was near 10 below, so in desperation I turned and followed my tracks back into the spruce. Like a wounded animal, instinct seemed to direct me to shelter. I had crossed an old fallen tree on the trail, unusually large for that area. I broke limbs from the tree and built a big fire next to the old trunk where it would be sheltered from the wind. Taking my ax, I cut young spruce and formed a large "U" with the fire at the top, and piled spruce boughs on the snow inside the "U". With the fire burning big, I pulled off all my clothes and dried them. My back side would freeze while my front side cooked. I was cold. I crawled into my sleeping bag and dropped off to sleep.

The late dawn of winter came slowly. I rolled my sleeping bag near the bed of coals, and without getting out I stirred the fire to life. Soon the blaze was almost cheerful, and I realized some of the swelling had left my eyes, but even in the dim light of dawn my eyes hurt when any light was allowed to strike them. I dressed quickly in the warm clothes hanging on the sticks around the fire. My mukluks appeared to have dried completely, and the dry socks felt warm and secure to my feet after hopping around on the frozen spruce boughs to get dressed.

The six miles into town were slow, painful miles. Without snowshoes, and unable to see, it took over four hours, without stopping to rest. I didn't know that day, but it would be weeks before I left the cabin again except to empty the honey bucket or purchase food supplies. After a week in the darkened house, my eyes were no longer swollen. The pain was gone most of the time, but any bright light stabbed like rods of iron into my sensitive, film-covered eyes. My vision never cleared that winter. Everything continued to look milky most of the time, but with the coming of spring there was too much freight to be moved to go outside to a doctor. The early freeze-up was causing hardship in most of the mining camps and in the town of Takotna. Freight was being dragged overland by caterpillar and dog team to relieve the stranded camps. I was a freighter; half-blind as I was, I went to work, too.

Trying to ignore the visual difficulty and pain of light on my eyes, I began taking contracts to move freight. From early spring, all through the summer, I continued working with limited vision. I had purchased a second truck, and the backlog of freight kept both vehicles operating long hours each day.

Winter arrived as slowly in the fall of 1940 as it had rapidly the previous year. November came before I was persuaded by my two brothers to go to a doctor in Nampa, Idaho, before I lost my vision completely.

The operation was relatively simple to remove the film from my eyes caused by the snowblindness, but now I required glasses and would always be sensitive to glare or bright light.

With my vision restored, Bill Pruitt and I decided to go back to O.K. creek and drill for gold. A successful miner agreed to loan us his rig on a 50-50 basis. If anything good showed up, the miner would finance a dredge to work the creek. The equipment was on skids and we pulled it along the same trail I had stumbled along while blinded by the snow. When we came to the boulder-strewn mountain that seemed to guard O.K. creek from outsiders, a battle of strength and wits began. The tractor, belonging to Rex Brown, now a third partner, was used to operate a system of blocks and tackle to inch the heavy unit up the mountain. At last, the drill was in place, and it seemed the gods guarding the gold of O.K. creek had been beaten.

Our method was to drill a series of holes across the creek, down to bedrock. As the slurry was forced from the hole, we would take samples and pan it to determine the amount of gold. When the opposite bank was reached, we would move the rig a hundred feet downstream and repeat the process.

The gods of Joaquin mountain laughed at our labors on O.K. creek. Hole after hole presented the same results—color, but no gold of quantity. I thought we had made peace with the mountain since the gold was not there, but the gods were not to be denied their revenge.

I was the strongest man on the trail of the three who worked the rig on O.K. creek. Naturally, they concluded, it was my job to pack the food and fuel from town to keep the operation going. This meant at least two trips each week, one for food and the other for gasoline. The frozen gravel eventually dulled the drill bit; an extra bit was put in place to continue operation while I packed the old bit into Takotna to be sharpened. The bit was four feet long and weighted nearly 80 pounds.

I strapped on my snowshoes, heaved the packboard with the drill bit onto my back and started for town. The trip had become routine. I would stop only once on the trail because of the cold and the tightening of muscles if I stayed too long to rest. As I walked into the machinist's shop, he whistled a long, low whistle.

"Did you pack that thing in from Joaquin mountain?" he said.

"Yeah, it got dull. Can you get it sharpened so I can leave in the morning?" I said as he helped me lower the packboard. With the weight lifted from my aching shoulders, I flexed my arms trying to restore circulation. Over five feet of snow had fallen that winter and even for a man as strong as I was it was a backbreaking chore to snowshoe 17 miles with so much weight.

Leaving early the next morning, all went well for me until I reached my resting point about half way to the drill site. I stopped at the usual tree stump on which I always rested, slid forward enough to rest the weight of the drill on the tree and allowed my shoulders to go back into place. The heavy drill extended well above my head; I am only 5' 6½". My muscles needed a rest before climbing Joaquin mountain. The temperature had dropped to 30-below zero before I left Takotna; I knew I must not rest long.

Standing to shift the weight evenly on my shoulder straps, one of them needed to be closer to my neck; I jumped slightly to suspend the weight of the drill while I shifted the strap. As I performed this maneuver, the top-heavy drill swung off balance, causing me to cross one snowshoe over the other to regain balance. I stumbled and lunged forward, face down into the snow. The weight of the bit took me all the way to the bottom of the five feet of snow, pinning me on the frozen moss beneath. The powdery snow came down around my face, and I panicked momentarily. Struggling to get air, I realized I was able to breathe in the loose snow. My self-control returned, and I began to methodically go about trying to get free. The snowshoes kept my feet suspended high above my head, and the weight of the drill bit was too much to lift from that position. For a moment it seemed the gods of Joaquin mountain would win the last round. Gradually, the back and forth muscle movement of my right shoulder worked the strap nearer to my arm. I slipped my shoulder free, and then inched from under the bit and packboard until I could sit upright—with my feet still above my head. I unstrapped the snowshoes and stood up. It was good to see the trees again. Joaquin mountain didn't seem like much of a climb when I thought where I could still be with a little less help from Someone who cared more for me than did the gods of that cursed hill.

Winter wore into spring slowly that year, and the backbreaking operation continued, but gold eluded us. As break-up came, we began the block and tackle process all over again to get the drill out of O.K. creek before the flats thawed and made travel impossible. The gods of Joaquin mountain had won after all; the old-timer's gold of O.K. creek had more reality when dreamed by a warm stove on a long winter night. Or else it is still there waiting for the friendship of the gods to change.

While I was outside for my eye operation, I travelled to Los Angeles and contacted Glen Carrington, a supplier of heavy equipment to the miners in Alaska. I had freighted much of the freight Carrington had shipped into the Takotna area. I explained the claims I had on O.K. creek and Gaines creek to the elder Mr. Carrington.

"I need a dozer, sluiceboxes, and all the equipment to mine these operations, but I don't have a dime right now," I explained. The old man thought for a long moment as he looked me squarely in the eye.

"McRoberts, you have a good reputation in those parts, don't ruin it now," he said. I sat silently, not sure what the old man meant, then Carrington continued, "You just order what you need and pay me when you can." Now the relentless search on Gaines creek could begin as it had on O.K. creek.

Mike McRoberts ran the Gaines creek camp, Bill Pruitt, probably the best driller in western Alaska, ran the drill. My brother, Dallas, had taken the manager's job of the N.C. Store when I entered the freight business. Each of us poured every cent we made back into the mining operation.

I leased other claims, and bought several more on Gaines creek, closer to Takotna and the Ophir fields. None ever produced much gold—nor the problems of the O.K. creek.

The Japanese attack on Pearl Harbor was followed by the invasion of the Aleutian Islands. War was coming close to Takotna, and the government was calling every able bodied man to arms. Dallas perished in a fire in July that destroyed the N.C. Store at Ophir creek.

The summer of '42 was no picnic for the men of the mining venture in Takotna. Pruitt was drafted in July and I lost my extra truck driver in August to the Army. I had to park one truck; all able bodied men were leaving. By fall, the government was closing all mining operations; I owed Carrington over $30,000 when I got my draft call from Uncle Sam.

I began to liquidate my assets to pay as many debts as possible before I became Private McRoberts on $21 a month. My mother had died, and my father was in the an Idaho hospital. Mike left as soon as the mining closed; someone had to take care of our father in Idaho and Mike had family responsibilities to think about. We closed the Gaines creek operation, and I began to sell the equipment. There wasn't much market for it, but eventually I had disposed of everything but the trucks. I continued to haul freight and square accounts. The year seemed to become one disaster after another for me.

In late August I received my notice from the Selective Service in Fairbanks. I didn't ignore the draft call, I just didn't answer it immediately. I continued to haul the backlog of freight, and put every spare dollar on the huge debt that seemed larger instead of smaller as the summer passed. With the freight hauled and fall coming, I sold both trucks and prepared to leave. I was still $10,000 short. I had scraped so hard to square accounts, I forgot to retain enough capital to get out of Takotna.

I had become a born again believer through the witness of Ethyl Peasgood in the spring of 1937. I became a strong believer in God's protection through many close calls. I told a friend that I just knew something would work out for me. God had never let me down and He knew I sure needed to get to Fairbanks.

The next day I was walking down the dirt street in Takotna and one of the fellows from a mining camp met me. The first thing he said was: "Ted, ya got enough money to get to the army on?" When I told him no, he reached into is pocket and loaned me enough for the plane fare to Fairbanks. I have never ceased to give God credit for that transportation money along with His watchful care.

CHAPTER VI

THE MARSHAL'S BADGE

The pilot agreed to fly from Takotna to Bethel before returning to Fairbanks—if he could see the cash first. I loaded my pack in the tiny plane and climbed into the right front seat. Dust rose from the gravel strip as the pilot applied full throttle and lifted the tail of the little red Bellanca. In the half circle turn toward Bethel, I looked down on the tiny world that had been *The Kusko Times*, my snowblindness, river freighting and mining claims. All of it had been good, but the best thing that had happened to me was the night I interviewed the attractive schoolteacher for *The Kusko Times* more than five years before.

Ethyl Peasgood was teaching in Bethel now; it was very important to me to see her one last time before answering my draft call. The draft would keep a few more days—I was already over a month late. The war looked as if it might last a long time; in 1942 it appeared everyone was winning but us. I felt the urgency of saying good-bye which might be forever, so Bethel was a necessary trip for me.

The pilot let me out without cutting the plane's engine. As soon as I had retrieved my pack, he pulled the door shut, waved his hand in a half-hearted salute, and left me standing in the blowing dust.

77

Swinging my pack onto one shoulder, I walked to the Bethel Roadhouse and got a room. I washed, changed clothes and splashed on a little shaving lotion, though I had shaved that morning.

In 1942, Bethel was a village of about 600 residents, not counting the Army Base across the river of 1,500 soldiers. The streets were dirt and everyone walked more than they rode. The few vehicles in town were not used for "draggin' main street" when the sun went down on Saturday night.

The late October evening was crisp and inviting as I stepped from the doorway of the Roadhouse and walked toward the little three-teacher schoolhouse. Above the school were two apartments. Ethyl lived in one, and the principal and his wife lived in the other. I stopped at the bottom of the outside stairs, smoothed my hair, then climbed the steps two at a time. I knocked a familiar knock that sort of said to the one inside that Ted McRoberts was in town. There was no answer. Knocking again I eased open the door very slowly and said, "Hello." A hoarse whisper came from the semi-darkness, "Come on in, I'm in here." Ethyl was in bed sick, resting after having taught school all day. I pulled up a chair and sat down beside the bed.

"You sound pretty sick to me," I said, "have you been to the doctor?"

"Lands no, you don't go running to the doctor with every cold and sniffle, besides it's just tonsillitis," Ethyl replied.

Her throat was so sore she hadn't eaten for several days because of the difficulty in swallowing. I asked her to let me look at her throat. One look sent a chill over my body. I had nursed my brother through diptheria years before, the yellow color of her swollen throat was enough to convince me she had the same thing. There was one other case of the disease in Bethel, I had heard earlier at the roadhouse.

"Lay still, don't move, I'll be right back," I called as I disappeared through the front door. Outside it was still light enough to see but too dark not to use lights. The Bethel hospital and doctor's residence was about a mile from the school. I started in that direction, hoping to find someone to give me a ride. About a block down the street, a pair of headlights appeared behind me then pulled to a stop.

"Need a lift?" the voice called.

I turned to get into the pickup and realized the driver was the town doctor.

"Doc, you've got to come with me to Ethyl's house, I think she has diptheria," I said as I climbed into the truck. He turned the truck around and headed for the school faster than he normally drove.

One look and the doctor turned to me, "Let's get her into my truck and to the hospital. I think you are probably right."

I had never been immunized against the disease, but I seemed to have a natural immunity. I never caught diptheria from my brother nor from Ethyl.

Someone had to teach the first four grades of the Bethel school while the teacher was in the hospital. I elected myself and went to the principal the next morning and offered to fill in for a few days. The delighted principal showed me a room full of children and backed toward the door, as if he were afraid I would turn and follow him.

Ethyl responded immediately to the serum for diptheria, coughing the yellow phlem daily until her throat was back to normal. I faithfully returned each morning to the noisy classroom that always grew strangely quiet when I entered and then as if on cue, responded in unison, "Good morning, Mr. McRoberts, when will Miss Ethyl be back?" They were delightful, well-disciplined children and *Mistah McRoberts* (as some of the younger ones called me) taught all the classes for two weeks. I would have taught longer, but a wire came from my brother, Mike, in Fairbanks, where he was waiting for space on a plane to Seattle. The wire said, REPORT TO FAIRBANKS IMMEDIATELY OR WARRANT WILL BE ISSUED FOR YOUR ARREST FOR EVADING DRAFT. The finality of it was convincing; I decided to go.

Mike had been delayed in Fairbanks because the only flights were crowded with military personnel. In 1942, the connecting air link with Seattle was the Pan American DC-3 which had to gas-up at Whitehorse, Juneau, and Ketchkan before arriving in Seattle. Fairbanks was small, and word was passed to Mike to reach me if he knew how.

I read the wire and a grin appeared on my face. I wondered which would be worse, getting drafted or arrested? I sent a wire to the Selective Service office in Fairbanks: JUST WAIT STOP WILL REPORT AS SOON AS POSSIBLE STOP NOT EVADING DRAFT STOP. Nothing more was said. Ethyl soon returned to her classroom and I packed for the last leg of the journey before losing the freedom of prospector-freighter I had enjoyed in bush Alaska.

The plane landed at Weeks Field in Fairbanks and taxied to the hanger-terminal of the Pacific Alaska Airlines. I walked the ten blocks downtown and went directly to the third floor of the Federal building and the

Selective Service office. I said to the girl behind the desk, "I'm Ted McRoberts and I'm answering the call you sent me two months ago. I'm ready now."

The girl smiled and said, "Just a moment Mr. McRoberts and I'll get your records." She went to a large gray file cabinet and began to thumb through the folders. Selecting one, she returned to her desk and began to read it. "Mr. McRoberts, since we contacted you the draft age has changed and you are too old for the draft. You will be forty in a few weeks and you don't have to answer now. Thirty-nine and one-half is the limit."

I stood there for a moment, waiting for the realization of what she said to take effect before I told her I had disposed of everything and got ready for this call. "I sold everything I had and walked away from what I couldn't sell and I have nothing to go to now. I want to go down with the Army."

"I'm sorry, Mr. McRoberts, but you can't even join," she replied sweetly.

I turned and walked out of the office without another word. Directly across the hall was the office of United States Marshal, Joe McDonald, Fourth Judicial District, an old friend of mine.

Alaska was a territory until 1959, and law enforcement was by U.S. Marshal and his deputies. The powerful jobs were secured by political appointment, and charged with the responsibility of keeping the peace over a land mass one-fifth the size of the entire United States. The Marshal appointed deputies to help police the vast reaches of the arctic in the Fourth Judicial District for which Fairbanks was the headquarters.

Special training was not required to become a U.S. Marshal, or a Deputy U.S. Marshal, in the sense of an academy or school. Usually the men were experienced in some manner to qualify them, but the one requirement to be a Deputy U.S. Marshal was at least three years experience in handling the public. The job did require, by unwritten law, a special breed of men. Men who could remain cool under difficult circumstances, and men who were physically able to withstand the demands of being in the bush. This special breed of "bush marshal" was a person who could communicate with people, native or white, recognize a lawbreaker and then be able to solve the situation. Sometimes it meant finding a solution without making an arrest. Often it meant hardships and dangers; sometimes it meant being a psychologist and counselor. Above all, it meant being a man who could walk tall among his peers with the respect of being a man before he was a marshal.

Marshal McDonald had often tried to get me to work for the Marshal's office but, I never felt qualified for the job. Once, during the slack winter months when I was visiting Ethyl, I served as guard and deputy to Deputy Marshal Jim Brewster's office in Bethel. I knew the country of the Kuskokwim better than most natives. For 300 miles in any direction, my name was known; I had walked into most of the camps selling *The Kusko Times* or carrying mining equipment. My physical feats had become legendary around the pot-bellied and smoke-filled rooms of Western Alaska. I found it difficult to believe that tales could become so distorted or grow so much with repetition.

I was small in size, 5' 6½'' and 140 pounds, when I walked across the hall that October in 1942 and entered the Marshal's office. Marshal McDonald was busily shuffling papers on his cluttered desk when I walked in and said, "Well, Joe, how about it, have you got a job for me?"

Without a greeting or a moment's hesitation Joe replied, "I have three, one in McGrath, one at Nulato and one at Bethel...take your choice."

"Well, I don't want to go to a place that's dead. I'll take the one at Bethel," I said.

The marshal at Bethel had the responsibility for 10,000 people scattered over western and southwestern Alaska. Brewster, the deputy there, was transferring to Ft. Yukon. When I worked briefly for him as a guard one winter, I learned as much in those brief months as most men learn in years on the force. Brewster was a West Point graduate and noted for his toughness. He knew criminal law and had learned the street scene as a policeman on skidrow in Seattle. He had been a policeman in Portland, Oregon and a Washington State Patrolman before coming to Alaska. When Brewster recognized I was interested in law enforcement, he did everything he could to train me. Neither of us suspected that I would wear the badge of the law in Bethel after he was gone.

Before anyone could become a Deputy U.S. Marshal, they had to be investigated. Marshal McDonald sent me back to Bethel as guard and assistant to Brewster until the investigation was completed. The rest of that fall and winter I worked under the rough tutelage of Brewster. Brewster rode hard to knock away the rough edges and prepare me as a new Deputy. On February 13, 1943, I became Deputy U.S. Marshal Ted McRoberts, and Brewster was sent to his new post in Ft. Yukon.

The sign on the door of the log jail on the banks of the Kuskokwin river was changed to reflect the transition and the metamorphosis was complete. The feeling deep inside of me had been there only once before. Seven years had passed since I had arrived in Anchorage and somehow I knew I had found my land. The same feeling was there again, this time I had found my job. I must admit it is a long way from the sheep camp in Idaho to the log jail in Bethel, but somehow, it was like arriving home after a long absence.

CHAPTER VII

CALL OF THE GREAT LAND

I never questioned my ability to do anything; I just never let it occur to me that failure could come. A new feeling swept over me the day Marshal Brewster climbed aboard the mail plane and headed for Ft. Yukon—a feeling of inadequacy I did not like. The new marshal's badge didn't carry with it a book on how to escape the empty gut feeling that said all the decisions of the office now rested on my shoulders. The feeling must be similar to that of a man on his first solo airplane flight. The thrill is shortlived when, speeding down the runway, he eases back on the controls and feels the lift of the wings as the plane leaves mother earth. He's flying all by himself! He climbs to altitude, banks left and stays in the pattern—then the moment of truth! If the plane gets safely back to earth it must be done by him, and him alone. There is no instructor to correct for an error in judgement. I felt that aloneness as I watched Brewster's plane disappear.

All these thoughts were uppermost in my mind as I opened the door to the Marshal's office that was to be my office for the next ten years.

The first few days after Brewster left were so peaceful I had little to do. I cared for the few prisoners in the jail, walked the town to keep an eye on activities, but for the most part, no one called on the Marshal. I feel sure it wasn't a lack of trust, it was just the newness of change and a fortunate twist of luck that allowed me to get used to wearing the Marshal's shoes.

Three days after the sign on the door was changed to bear my name, I was walking through the village streets and passed a stranger cutting wood. By nature I am friendly and like to meet strangers, but as marshal it was also part of my job. I stopped and chatted with the young man. He was from a tundra village about 50 miles from Bethel and had come to town to await his entrance into the tuberculosis hospital located about a mile out in the country. His lungs were not so bad that he could not work, but the doctor felt he should be in the hospital for a month to be thoroughly checked. I knew the family for whom the man was working, so I thought little of the incident.

Early the next morning the constant knocking on the front door sounded like trouble itself. As I opened the door, an old native man began to talk so fast I could not determine what he wanted. I did recognize him as the Russian Catholic priest whose small church was located about 150 yards from where I had met the stranger cutting wood.

The Russian Catholics in the Kuskokwim were all natives—even their priests. They traced their origin to the days of the Russian occupation of Alaska before the United States purchased the territory from Russia in 1867. Most of them had no support and were a struggling group of believers.

I invited the old priest inside and urged him to sit down and slow his speech so I could understand. The best I could determine in his excitement was that someone had broken into the church and stolen $80. All of the money was in twenty dollar bills, and belonged in their building fund. The tiny congregation had been saving for months to get enough money to build a new building and now someone had taken their treasured efforts.

I walked slowly beside the old priest as we started toward the church. Approaching the door of the church, I noticed an ax laying on the ground and the splintered door-jam was mute evidence to its use. Inside the church nothing else seemed out of place. Picking up the ax as I left, I assured the distraught priest I would do everything possible to find his money.

I asked the lady of the house, where I had seen the stranger cutting wood, if the ax belonged to her.

"Why, yes, it does," she said, "where did you get it. I thought the man cutting wood for me had stolen it."

"Is he here now?" I said.

"No, he was admitted to the hospital this morning, but now that I have my ax back everything's alright, isn't it Marshal?"

"Yes, ma'am, everything's fine," I told her as I left her house and walked the mile to the hospital.

Checking at the hospital to make sure the man was really a patient there, I then alerted the merchants in town to be on the lookout for anyone spending twenty dollar bills. Not many people in Bethel had twenty dollar bills in 1943.

I went to the U.S. Commissioner and got a warrant for the man's arrest, but I knew the circumstantial evidence was too weak to convict him, I would have to wait for more. Weeks passed without any word of twenty dollar bills being spent in Bethel, then one day an N.C. Co. worker hurried into my office with a word from his boss. A stranger has just been in the store and bought some groceries, he paid for them with a $20 bill. The clerk said he had seen other $20 bills in his billfold as the man withdrew the money. In their conversation, the stranger told the clerk he had been in the hospital but had chartered a plane to take him back to his village.

I grabbed the warrant and ran to the little building that served as an office for the airport. The only available transportation was a five place plane parked on the river ice. I chartered the plane and the pilot warmed the engine as we taxied to the end of the snow-packed strip.

We had gone about thirty-five miles from Bethel, when the faster, larger plane I had chartered closed the gap between the earlier chartered plane. We spotted the little plane landing on a frozen lake alongside a village. By the time I arrived, the small plane was airborn again and the pilots waved as our paths crossed.

Our plane taxied toward the shore and the dozen natives who had gathered to see why two planes would land at their village in such a short space of time. Climbing from the plane, I asked which house the man who had just arrived lived in, and was directed to the far side of the village.

Most of the village houses were built with logs and sod, half-buried in the ground, with only a single door opening. Without knocking, I walked right into the house; the man was counting out the money to his wife, among which lay three twenty dollar bills. I explained why I had come and that I had a warrant for the man's arrest; I took all the money in as evidence. Under great protest, the stranger returned to Bethel and took up residence in the little log jail.

All night long I questioned the angry prisoner. Time and again he would tell me where he had gotten the money and each story had a different flaw in it. I would confront him with the lie and the man would tell another story. I knew the villagers didn't have that kind of money, and the coincidence of that denomination of bills was sufficient odds to continue my questioning. By morning the man confessed to taking the money.

The charge of breaking and entering increased the charge to a felony; the taking of the money was a misdemeanor. We only charged him with the lessor offense so we could try him in Bethel. He was convicted and sent to Fairbanks to serve six months in jail.

I took the three twenty dollar bills and headed for the little Russian Catholic church. All the way over there I kept remembering how much the money had meant to the old priest trying to build his new house of God. When the old man came to the door, I handed him $80 and told him I was sure glad we got all his money back for the church. The elated priest almost shook my arm off. I never told him that the spent cash had been made up out of my own pocket. The people only knew I had done my first job well and that pleased me most of all.

Any marshal in the north country must have a keen eye, a natural gift of suspicion and a lot of luck to be detective, homicide chief, peacemaker, or whatever the need dictates.

By the time Spring came in Bethel, the February appointment as marshal seemed so far in the past that I felt I had always been a marshal. The weather was warming in the daytime, but snow remained deep on the ground. The powdery flakes of the cold winter had turned to the moist, heavy snow of spring, and the warm days added to the firmness of the hard-packed snow.

Early one morning, a knock on the door of the log jailhouse again had the urgent sound of trouble. Even though I had been marshal only two months, I had learned to interpret the gentle rap of a friendly visit, the hurried knock of fear, the banging of the late-night drunk, and the firm, rapid knock of a person in trouble. This knock is the rapid knocking of someone in trouble, I thought, as I opened the door to the excited manager of the Northern Commercial Company store, the largest store in our little delta town.

"Come with me, Marshal, the store was broken into last night and we were robbed," he said.

Once inside the store the thief, or thieves had taken only money; the manager remembered one of the bills was a $50 bill because it was the first he had seen in Bethel. Nothing else in the crowded store seemed disturbed as I walked through with the manager. Noticing one window unlocked, on a hunch I raised the window and looked at the snow beneath; a surge of excitement raced through me as I saw tracks of a person in the snow leading away from the building but none coming toward the building. I walked outside to a place below the window and looked closely at the tracks; the tread of the boot-track was unusual.

I couldn't remember seeing a boot-track like that anywhere around Bethel before. I asked the manager to get me a big shovel. He was so excited in his state of confusion he obeyed. Taking the shovel, I carefully scooped up the snow track and put it in cold storage inside the N.C. Company store.

Weeks passed and the track never appeared anywhere else in Bethel. The snow was gone and the dusty streets offered little chance of finding a boot to match the frozen track I had in the cold storage locker at the store.

One night, as I casually made my rounds to check the town before going to bed, I walked into the Tundra Shack, a small ice cream parlor where young people usually gathered in the evenings. As I chatted with the young people, I was introduced to a new boy from Fairbanks. After the initial greeting, the boy sat down at one of the tables and crossed his legs. His action caused my eyes to turn in his direction. I couldn't believe what I saw; there was the same tread on the boy's boot that was frozen in the snow at the N.C. Co. store!

Circumstantial evidence is not enough to convict a man—especially an imprint of a similar boot track taken weeks before the thawing spring snow, I thought.

I left the ice cream parlor without a word to the young man. I began to inquire around town about the new boy. The smooth arrest in the first case I had faced had gained me respect. My friendship with the people had gained me their trust and they talked freely to me about the young man. The boy had been in trouble in Fairbanks, but little else was known. I passed the word that if he tried to leave town, I was to be notified.

Days passed quietly and nothing seemed to change. One day a plane arrived from Bristol Bay. The youth contacted the pilot and arranged passage. A native boy overheard the conversation and hurried to my office. I thanked the boy and asked him not to say anything to anyone. Getting a warrant didn't take long in Bethel; I hurried to the U.S. Commissioner's office and swore a warrant for the young man. When the pilot and the boy arrived at the plane I was leaning against the wing strut.

"Howdy, Marshal," the pilot said, "you going to Bristol Bay with us?"

"No, I have a warrant for your passenger though," I said. Serving the warrant, I began to search the young man's pack. Among the personal things I found some checks, a few bills, and the $50 bill taken from the N.C. Company store weeks before. Confronted with the evidence, the youth confessed and was taken before the Bethel Commissioner's court. He was bound over to the grand jury in Fairbanks, and I had solved my second robbery case.

My reputation as a marshal spread fast after this second robbery case was solved. The frozen boot track seemed a strange method to most who heard the story; people began to say the new marshal had help from God, and I would have been the first to make that confession.

Reputation is often better than fact and I used my good fortune with a rifle to excellent advantage as a marshal. Three events happened over a period of five years that made good stories in the camps and cabins during the winter when talk was more in abundance than work.

When I was in Takotna, my reputation for endurance had earned me a job for the N.C. Company as the man to repair the telephone line from McGrath through Takotna to Ophir Creek. The line was built on tri-pods and moose had knocked portions of it down. The line crossed swamp country and mosquitoes would swarm so thick I often would go under the waist-deep water just to get away from them for brief moments. The trip took all day and most of the night to make the 17 difficult miles that placed me on the opposite bank of the Kuskokwim from the trading post at McGrath. Wet and chilled to the bone, I looked at the wide, lazy river; not a boatman in sight nor a sign of life. I had arrived at an abandoned sawmill, but I was too wet and tired to start a fire. Realizing someone would soon be checking their fish nets, I buried myself in a pile of sawdust. As my body warmed I fell asleep.

The sound of an outboard motor sent sawdust flying when I jumped from my burrow and ran to the river's bank. Coming up the middle of the river was a single fishing boat; I waved frantically until the boat turned and headed toward me.

"Friend, I sure need to get across the river, I'll be glad to pay," I told the boatman.

"If you will wait until I check my nets, I'll take you there for nothing. Climb aboard," the native man said.

Arriving at the trading post, I walked in on a breakfast conversation between Dave Clough, an old-timer who had owned the original roadhouse in McGrath, and his friend, Mitchell, a Takotna trader. Mitchell bought his supplies from the retail store in McGrath, hauled them back to Takotna and resold them with the added cost for transportation added on. The trip was a 65 mile river run in the summer and 17 miles overland in the winter.

Dave turned the sourdough pancakes and told me to quit dripping water on the floor. Underneath the chair where I was sitting, a puddle of water had formed as it seeped from my wet clothing. I apologized and told him of my twenty-four hour walk through the swamp without sleep, except for the brief nap in the sawdust pile. He didn't say anymore about the puddle of water.

As Mitchell loaded his long, flat-bottomed riverboat with supplies, I asked if I could ride back to Takotna with him.

"Sure you can, but you've got to promise you won't sleep all the way," he said jokingly.

About forty miles from McGrath, as the boat struggled against the current to reach Takotna, I looked up river and saw a lone goose coming toward us near the middle of the river and about 30 feet above the water. Mitchell had his rifle in the boat, I picked it up and swung with the goose as he passed us. The shot echoed along the river above the noise of the outboard, but Mitchell's yell was louder than either noise when the goose tumbled into the river. I laid the gun down as if nothing unusual had happened and Mitchell swung the boat around to pick up the goose. Mitchell must have told the story a hundred times after that, each time the accuracy and uncanny shooting became more legendary.

The second incident again involved Mitchell and only served to put frosting on the already embellished story of the lone goose.

Mitchell had gone with me to Sterling Landing, a point on the Kuskokwim where boats could be unloaded if they could not navigate the Takotna river. My freighting business was booming now and Mitchell went along for the trip as I hauled a load of freight from the landing site. I had built a small log cabin at the landing to enable me to spend the night there if necessary. We stayed in the cabin this trip after loading the cargo. Early the next morning, we began the slow trip over the rough road back to Takotna. Snow had fallen lightly during the night, and as we began the creeping climb over a long hill, I spied fresh moose tracks coming out of the brush and leading up the road ahead of us.

"Look there," I said to Mitchell, "boy, I'll bet we see that guy around the next turn. If we do you grab this hand brake and hold it hard, it won't stay by itself, and I'll jump out and we'll get us a moose."

Sure enough around the next bend the big bull was walking up the middle of the road. Mitchell grabbed the brake, and I grabbed the rifle, and the moose grabbed for cover as he trotted out of sight. I ran up the road; around the turn I saw the big fellow jump on a cutbank about four feet high. I was still in sight of Mitchell when I swung the rifle to my shoulder and fired almost instantly. The bullet broke the bull's neck about a foot behind his head and he fell to the edge of the road. By the time Mitchell finished with that story my reputation was secure.

The third incident was another one-in-a-million shots that spread fame far more than fact, and helped to cement my reputation as a straight shooting Marshal, if the need ever arose.

I had been the law along the Kuskokwim for about 18 months when it became necessary for me to make a circuit to Nelson Island and across to Nunivak Island. The Moravian missionary freight boat was supplying the natives along the river's mouth, so I secured permission to ride with them.

The delta area was filled with ducks, and as the slow boat moved through the nearly still water, ducks would scare and fly past the boat. A mallard on the wing can be difficult to hit with a shotgun and almost impossible with a .22 rifle. The native crew had amused themselves most of the morning by trying to shoot a duck on the wing with a .22 rifle. Finally tiring of the impossible sport that had not yielded one duck, they laid the rifle on some cargo and started below. I casually picked up the rifle and looked it over. The native men began to mumble and laugh about the Marshal shooting a duck. I was always ready for a challenge, but more for a joke I aimed at an oncoming duck and squeezed the trigger. The spat of the .22 could barely be heard above the noise of the boat, but there was no mistake as the mallard fell into the sea.

90

I turned as casually as I had begun and laid the gun back on the cargo. Trying not to smile, I acted as if it was all in a day's work.

At every stop the excited natives reenacted the shot that was heard along the Kuskokwim when Marshal McRoberts so easily dropped the flying mallard—truly the stories they had heard must be true. I never let it be known I really wasn't that good.

My biggest challenge as the new marshal on the Kuskokwim came when the natives began complaining that no salmon were running in the river. When I questioned fishermen about the odd phenomenon I found it wasn't as odd as I thought. Word had spread along the native grapevine that a fishing vessel had stretched gill nets across the mouth of the river and was netting most of the run of king salmon. There was nothing in the manual to tell a marshal how to arrest a fifty foot trawler in the middle of a river!

Most of the night I tossed and turned in my bed trying to decide the best course of action. Sometime after the clock struck three the solution came—rent a plane and arrest the boat; with that decided I went to sleep.

Early the next morning, I strapped on my gun and pinned on my marshal's badge. Chartering a float plane, I had another stop to make before we flew to the trawler anchored in the river. I dropped Ethyl at Fortuna Lodge on the Yukon River where she had made arrangements to take the Alaska S.S. Nenana to the headwaters of the Yukon and float down the river. After this side trip, we headed for the fishing vessel and circled overhead several times before landing. The pilot taxied near enough for me to climb the ladder and board the vessel. The ship seemed deserted as I walked across the deck calling to anyone who might hear. Eventually, the cook heard the commotion on deck and came topside to investigate.

"Where's the crew for this vessel?" I asked.

"They are all out fishing. Who wants to know?" the cook replied.

"I'm the U.S. Marshal, and I am placing this boat and its crew under arrest, beginning with you," I said.

As each dory returned to the mother ship, I informed the crew they were under arrest and were not to leave the ship. When the skipper came on board, I again identified myself, and informed him that his 16 man crew was under arrest and his boat was in custody of the U.S. Marshal; they must weigh anchor and go upstream to Bethel where they would be formally charged.

The boat was out of Oregon, and the skipper tried to convince me they were not doing anything illegal, even though the hold was half full of fresh salmon and the nets still in the water. The argument didn't last long for the mouth of the river was not open to any commercial fishing.

In the Commissioner's court in Bethel, a decision had to be made. If we fined the skipper more than $1,000 the case would be bound over to Fairbanks in which instance the crew would be held and the fish would spoil in the refrigerated hold. After due deliberation, the court fined the skipper $1,000 and allowed him to keep his fish if he never came into those waters again. The delighted skipper headed downriver with a wave of his arm that expressed a gratitude beyond words. That is the only warrant I ever got against a ship on the high seas, but the salmon began to fill the river immediately and it seemed a warrant well taken by all involved.

CHAPTER VIII

THE MARSHAL AND THE MILITARY

Fifteen hundred soldiers isolated along the Kuskokwim, with a native village across the river selling liquor and women, would make the bravest Marshal tremble.

The jail averaged about a dozen prisoners at all times during the war years, sometimes as high as 29 prisoners were crowded into the tiny log structure. I was charged with keeping the peace and operating the jail as the U.S. Deputy Marshal at Bethel. I was allowed three guards to keep the jail around the clock, the rest was up to me. The government allowed per diem to feed the prisoners. Usually one of the prisoners did the cooking as part of the chores, while another would be charged with emptying the honey bucket - there was no sewage system in Bethel. Before the war most of the prisoners were Eskimos and half-breeds, a few whites occasionally. But in the early 1940's not many whites lived in southwestern Alaska—except, of course, the military. As Marshal at Bethel, I was the only law enforcement agent in a radius of 250 miles.

My job was complicated by military on leave. Bethel was also a port for ocean-going boats as large as 4000 tons. Army boats, Merchant Marine boats, fishing boats, cargo boats and the river steamers all put into Bethel.

Bethel had a lot of liquor stores. It seemed everybody who sold anything also sold liquor. There were several bars along the streets of this dusty delta town which seemed to dispense liquor from their early morning opening until closing time at night.

Frequently it was difficult to get the supplies the populace needed, for when the boats were loaded, the liqour cargo was loaded first, which left little room for other things. Weekends usually meant that I didn't take off my clothes from Friday morning until the last soldier was on the 10 o'clock curfew boat back across the river.

Bethel Army Base had many men of the Air Corps stationed there. They flew missions over the Aleutians and were charged with stopping the Japanese advance on the western coast of Alaska. Security was tight. Bethel was blacked out at night; during the long winter nights this made winter seem a time of perpetual darkness. The black-outs made law enforcement more difficult too.

Of the 10,000 Eskimos in the radius of my jurisdiction, very few of them had had much contact with white men. Most of that contact had been with traders or the few miners in the area, never anything like the mass number of military that flooded Bethel during the war. The natives were frightened of the white soldier and his drunken antics; they seldom resisted in any way. Increasingly, the knock on my wooden jailhouse door became the knock of some scared native who had been run out of his own home by a soldier who had taken his woman.

At first, I would follow the man back to the cabin, arrest the soldier, and then turn him over to the military to prosecute. When trial came, I became the star witness on the stand to testify against the soldier. The army prosecutor would twist events and questions until I would look like the criminal for having arrested one of the great fighting men of the Armed Forces. The soldier would be turned loose with company punishment—or no punishment at all. In company punishment, the man is given extra duty for a period of time as punishment for his wrong doing. But it was usually nothing more than K.P.

After the sixth time of arresting a man only to have him go unpunished for a crime that would merit a prison sentence for a civilian, I decided to tighten the law in Bethel. I would arrest the criminal, file a complaint in the United States Commissioner's court in Bethel, sentence them in Bethel, and hold them in my jail. Being a federal officer, my jurisdiction was extensive, and the Commissioner backed my every request. Military

94

persons were not exempt from a U.S. Marshal, even in war-time.

The military was enraged. They threatened to take things to a higher authority, and did appeal through Anchorage to the District Attorney's department. They contended that such action deprived them of the use of the soldiers, which it did. But the D.A. ruled in my favor. Then the appeal was taken to Washington. Washington also upheld my action.

As soon as the Army saw it couldn't force me to release the soldiers through political pressure, they offered to cooperate with me. Ten men from the Infantry stationed at the Base were picked to serve as Military Police. They were hand-picked, large, even-tempered men. The town of Bethel furnished a place to lodge them in the Community hall and the Army sent a cook to provide for their meals. They were ten soldiers stationed in the township of Bethel, but under the jurisdiction of the U.S. Marshal whenever I needed them. This ended the "war" between the Marshal and the military, but not our problems.

The ten MPs were soon known to be rougher on their own men than I had ever been. Sometimes the evenings would burst open with mob fighting if the Infantry and the Engineers came to town on the same night. I would call for the MPs and they would wade into the melee with clubs swinging. One lick on the head put a man on the ground. Then the husky MP would pick up the unconscious soldier and toss him into the back of a waiting truck. When the "game" was over, the score was always in favor of the MPs. The MPs would then drive to the river bank, put their "cargo" on a boat and send them to the hospital on the Army base. Word soon spread throughout the delta. It wasn't long until the town settled down and only isolated incidents involved the Army.

The ten soldiers didn't patrol the streets with me; they served only as "deputies" when I called for them, which wasn't often. But when I needed help they were my salvation.

A boat load of soldiers came across to Bethel on a 24-hour pass in late October 1943. The soldiers were to be back on the Base the evening of the second day. But they had decided that they were going to have their "night on the town."

As I walked the streets that evening, an uneasy feeling seemed to tell me trouble was in the making. It was more than the rowdy noise in the bars and the few soldiers on the street already showing signs of too much liqour. Starting out for my second round of the evening, I met a native man who said a bunch of soldiers had a woman cornered down in the kasige (pronounced: kosh she gee) which was the public meeting house of the village. The structure was a large building, half buried in the ground and built of logs. Dome-shaped and covered with sod, it resembled a giant mud ball and was used as an entertainment center by the natives.

I walked into the building alone. Ten soldiers had the girl cornered and were drunk enough to abuse her. However, she was unharmed. I attempted to break up the group, but they turned on me instead. I backed against a wall and faced the ten armed and angry men. "Come on big lawman, pull your gun," one of them taunted.

"I don't have a gun, and don't need one for you," I bluffed as I worked my way toward the door.

The soldiers moved in closer as I talked fast and loudly about the mistake they were making. They were determined to take me apart by hand if I refused to be shot. As soon as I reached the door I ducked out into the night and waited in the street for the first one to come out. I figured I'd nail them one at a time as they came through the door. None came out, so I left to get the MPs.

Covering the quarter-mile distance to the quarters of my "soldier-marshals" didn't take long. I called them to get up, because I needed help. By the time we reached the kasige, the drunken soldiers had sobered enough to realize they had threatened a federal officer. They were nowhere in sight. Dividing into groups, we began a systematic search, first of the waterfront and then house by house. Some of the soldiers were caught stealing boats in an attempt to get back to the army base. Others were hiding in houses and buildings around town, but by morning all of them were arrested and in jail.

The Army had toughened its policy after I beat its appeals in Washington, D.C., and the ten arrested men were scared. I let them suffer their unknown fate throughout the day. The only law they had really broken, outside of threatening a federal officer, was of minor consequence to me. The girl had not been hurt, no boats were actually stolen. However, the soldiers in my jail knew they were in trouble with the army if the charges were made known. By late afternoon, the ten were extremely docile and repentant for their actions. After a stern lecture, I released them to the custody of the Military Police—without charges—but only minutes before their leave time was due to expire.

I believe my willingness to preserve law without malice is what gained me increasing respect in the delta country. Even with this respect

96

there were constant threats on my life and I always slept with a gun at the head of my bed, another under my pillow, and a third gun under the covers. In every arrest of G.I.s, even with my reputation for fairness, someone always threatened to kill me. The respect of the U.S. Marshal's badge, however, carried great weight and often I could make arrests without the help of the MPs—especially when outsiders came to Bethel.

A Merchant Marine vessel came into port with military supplies and tied up at the Army docks across the river. Shore leave was the sailor's delight—even in Bethel. The Army had evening leave and also came to town. I knew it was going to be a busy night when I arrested the first drunk before most other men were drinking.

One honky tonk restaurant in Bethel consisted of a big hall on the edge of town. There was room for dancing and eating, but none ever called it a "high class place."

That night, the owner sent a runner to get me when some Merchant Marines began to break up the joint. When I arrived I found broken tables, debris on the floor, and the place in a mess. The men had taken over; some of them were serving drinks, others were waiting on tables and doing the cooking. Everything was free of course, and the crowd in the building was taking full advantage of the gracious nature of the drunk sailors.

I stood at the door for a moment to size up the situation, then yelled as loudly as I could to get their attention. When they realized I was the Marshal, the place grew strangely quiet. The sailors had been drinking heavily, but they knew the authority back of my Marshal's badge. I arrested all of them without any resistance. I lined them up and marched them into the darkened street without a word of protest. Since it was after midnight, most of the other places were closed. One of the sailors decided to run for it and broke from the ranks. I was after him immediately. The boy didn't know the town and fell head-long into a drainage ditch with me right on top of him; I handcuffed him before he could figure out what was happening. When I marched the "escapee" back to the group they were all standing in the darkness trying to see who won the race. When they saw I had succeeded in cuffing a man nearly twice my size, they decided to go to jail peacefully.

Their boat was due to sail at high tide, which was 2 a.m., and they were to be back on deck by 1:30 a.m.; it was now 12:30 a.m. I put all the men in one cell and told them I was going to file charges in the morning. They began to beg and plead, but I turned and walked out of the jail. The guard later told me how they had pleaded for him to convince me that if they could get back on their boat they would pay all damages and never come back to Bethel again. What they didn't know was where I was during their moments of anguish.

I left the jail and went to the home of some Eskimo friends who had boats. I hired them to bring their boats to the bank of the Kuskokwim directly below the jail, a distance of about thirty yards. About 1:15 a.m., I returned to the jail; the uproar of anguish began again. I told them to get quiet and then spent fifteen minutes scaring the daylights out of them for messing up my town. I held the men until 1:40 a.m., then released them without charges. Their ship was anchored about 400 yards off shore and they were marched to the waiting boats and taken directly to the ship. They were the happiest freed prisoners I ever saw in Bethel. Each man shook my hand and slapped my back, some later sent cards of thanks for my consideration.

Some people thought that a drinking G.I. on a weekend pass was a harmless fellow just letting off the pressure of being away from home, or a release from the regimentation of Army life. Some of the other stories are better left untold for I believe the strange manner of a few men should not reflect on the attitude of the whole. Occasionally, I had the pervert, the mental case, or the very mean to contend with in marshalling the military of Bethel.

Once, a big drinking party was planned at the home of one of the villagers. Many of the G.I.s were well-known in Bethel and trusted by the residents. A man and woman wanted to attend the party which was only a block down the street. They left their 10 month old baby with a G.I. friend who said he would babysit the child.

About midnight, the mother decided to go check on things at home. As she walked into the house the baby was screaming and the soldier was gone. Going into the bedroom, the mother screamed loudly enough to be heard a block away when she saw the blood-soaked child and bed. The soldier had attempted rape on the infant. She grabbed the baby in her arms and ran to my house screaming. I got out of bed. As I dressed, the woman told me the story and who had been babysitting for her. I walked the street asking if anyone had seen the man. Soon someone pointed out the direction he had gone. I knew the boy and some of his habits. He frequently visited another native family across the slough from the main part of town. When I arrived, the man was there and didn't resist arrest.

The night was pitch dark and rain had been falling until the streets of Bethel were a quagmire. To reach the jail, I and my prisoner had to pass in front of the house where the all-night drinking party was being held. The mother had left my office and gone to her husband at the party. The enraged husband had gotten his 30-06 rifle and returned to the party. When we crossed the road and started along the river bank, the husband came out of the house and yelled for us to stop and for me to give the man to him. I kept right on going as if I had not heard; I knew I would be a difficult target in the darkness if he started shooting. The first bullet came so close to my head I felt the wisp of air on my ear. We broke into a run as the man continued to fire at us. When we reached the jail, which had a storm entrance, I opened the door and shoved the soldier into the room and yelled for the guard to put the prisoner away. I then stepped back into the storm entrance behind the door. When the gunman came through the door I met him with a stiff left hook to the midsection. Before he could recover from the blow, I grabbed the rifle and strong-armed it away from him, then shoved him inside. As soon as the angry father got control of himself, I let him go without pressing charges.

The man's fury was not spent, however. He went back to the party, and other friends in town, to get help. They were going to break into the jail and take the soldier by force.

We barred the jail door and waited. The mob didn't materialize, but all through the night we could hear small groups trying to form themselves into a sufficient force to storm the jail. For some reason it took the military two days to remove the prisoner; neither I nor the guard left the jail for very long during that time. Tempers were running high in town and trouble seemed ready to start at any moment.

The military removed the soldier from the Bethel area, and inquiries as to his fate always were met with the same answer: "Wartime rape carries with it the death penalty." Nothing else was ever known. The child was taken to Anchorage and survived the ordeal without further difficulty.

Some people attribute their fortunate circumstances to fate, accident or luck. But since the first spring in Takotna, when the attractive schoolteacher convinced me that Jesus Christ should be the answer for my life, I have believed it was the hand of God helping me. For me being Marshal was as much being in God's will as being a preacher was to a minister. Many times a different move, a delayed reaction, a violent circumstance seemed to change just enough to save my life.

The mighty Kuskokwim river always became an uncontrollable force during spring break-up. My log jail on its banks seemed to get closer to destruction each year as the raging current cut more of the bank away. Finally, I decided the jail had to be moved. The N.C. Co. had a group of small rental houses with a board walk extending the full length in front of them. They were small, just a kitchen and bedroom, but I rented one as a home until the jail and quarters could be relocated.

In late fall, winter, and early spring, storms often come in Bethel. The rains come in torrents along the Bering seacoast and as far inland as Bethel; the cold rain and snow is often driven by gale-force winds. Some nights the weather was unbearable, but usually these nights meant I could get a good night's sleep. On one such miserable night, I turned in early, exhausted from a weekend of working long hours. The storm and early darkness seemed to bring a peace to the troubled town.

About midnight, I heard a scream from somewhere that brought me out of bed and into my clothes. I strapped on my gun and walked out into the heavy rain and wind. Standing in front of my house on the boardwalk, I listened. Not a sound. I looked in both directions; the town seemed asleep. Slowly, I walked down the boardwalk, my heels making the only sound except the noise of the storm. Down one side of the street to the end, walking as close to the houses as possible. If anyone was inside making trouble I wanted to hear it. Pausing for a moment at the end of the street, I turned and started up the other side, listening at each house. As I got even with my house, I saw somebody in the middle of road stomping something in the mud. Thinking the object must be the woman I heard scream, I ran toward the scene and turned on my flashlight. Standing in the muddy street was a huge Army Sergeant with his head and face covered with blood. His hands were dripping with blood and he was stomping my sleeping bag into the mud. Before the Sergeant could recover from the bright light in his eyes, I grabbed his arm and swung it behind him. A click of the handcuffs and the other arm was in place. The jail was just across the road; I awakened the guard and locked the blood-covered man in a cell to sleep off the liquor that had made him crazy.

Returning home, I noticed a bloody handprint on the sill of my front door. Inside, blood had dripped across the kitchen where another blood print was on the bedroom door. Then the bloody trail proceeded over to my bed. I breathed a prayer of relief. Had the man come in on me that way I would have shot him. The three guns I kept nearby were for just such emergencies, and I felt the threats on my life were justification for shooting.

The next morning my questioning and investigation revealed the story. The Sergeant had been in the little house next to mine playing poker. He got drunk and beligerant, but the man living there was as tough as he was. In the argument, the civilian hit the soldier over the head with a liquor bottle and cut his head about seven inches. This was when the woman screamed. By the time I dressed and got outside the soldier had left in a dazed condition and was wandering down the street. He decided to go back and kill the man who had hit him. Drunken and injured he got into the wrong house and came after me; all the houses look alike even in the daytime. When the bed was empty, the man grabbed what was there and dragged it into the street and began stomping it.

The big, likeable soldier was anybody's friend when he was sober, but given a little liquor he was mean. I didn't want to press charges if the man would agree to pay for the sleeping bag. I turned him over to the military without civilian charges, but he lost his stripes and was transferred from Bethel.

Not all trouble from across the river came in uniform. Stationed with the military was a civilian contingent of Civil Aeronautics Authority personnel. The C.A.A. was the forerunner of the Federal Aviation Administration, which controls air traffic within the continental limits of the United States.

I was standing in front of the jail watching the lazy rolling of the Kuskokwim river in the late August evening. The last rays of the vanishing sun were jumping from ripple to ripple, and the glow on the water seemed the perfect end to a perfect day. The calmness of the evening was broken only by the starting of an outboard motor across the river near the army base. I watched as the boat headed into the current and then turned to angle toward the spot where I was standing. The boat docked at the bank directly below me and a tall, young man climbed the bank.

"Marshal, they asked me to come and get you," he said, "some guy has gone berserk in his room and is shooting up the place."

"You go back and tell them I'll be there just as soon as I can make it. I need to get my gun and I'll come in my boat," I replied.

When I arrived at the C.A.A. housing area, I found the crowd stirring with excitement. Everyone was afraid to go into the building, or even close to it, for fear of being shot. The man had been in his upstairs room all day, yelling and screaming to the top of his voice. He would shoot until he emptied his pistol and then reload.

I slipped from building to building until I could inch along the outside wall of the bullet-riddled house. Slowly, I opened the front door and waited. All of the shots and screams were coming from upstairs; I entered quietly and climbed the stairs, careful not to make any sound. With my gun drawn and my back to the wall, I moved silently down the hallway until I was outside the room. Inside, the madman raved and cursed while firing shots until his gun was empty. Twice I counted six shots before the lull, then six shots more. The third volley was fired and I assumed he was ready to reload. Hitting the door with my shoulder, I burst into the room of the surprised gunman who had not heard me approach.

The half-clothed man, sitting in the middle of the bed hardly saw me as I sprang through the door and onto the bed. Bringing my pistol down hard on the arm of his gun hand, I sent the half loaded pistol flying across the room. Tossing my own gun on the bed, I pinned the man down before he could fully realize what had happened. Putting the handcuffs on him was almost an automatic motion, and the man just relaxed as if he was glad it was over.

Looking around the room carefully in order to file my report, I started to count the bullet holes, then realized there were hundreds of them. Pictures on the wall had been shot, those of people had holes in the middle of their forehead or in each eye. The man obviously knew how to handle his weapon.

I knew everyone in the C.A.A. camp, and they knew me. The man realized he was arrested by the Federal Marshal and calmed down; I took him to the Bethel jail. I saw immediately what was troubling the man; he had a severe case of dilerium tremens. He had been on an extended drunk, and when he began to sober, the creeping monsters started chasing him around the room. To defend himself from the creatures, the man shot them each time they moved. Considering the number of shots, they must have been extremely active monsters. The man was taken before the U.S. Commissioner's office and sentenced to serve his time in my little log jail.

CHAPTER IX

LIVING OFF THE COUNTRY

Robert Service immortalized the idea that only the strong survive in this land up north, but difficulty in survival was not always limited to gold-rush camps and bush justice.

Being Deputy U.S. Marshal in Bethel meant I must care for my personal needs and, if I had prisoners in jail, care for their needs also. The government allowed $2.25 per day to feed the prisoners I kept in my log jail on the Kuskokwim in the mid-1940's. I was a bachelor and, consequently, had no wife to bring meals to the prisoners, as the movies of the old west at the N.C. Co. Theatre usually depicted.

An avid gardener, I always produced more than I could use from my garden plot. My first year in Alaska marked the only year I failed to raise a garden. I was told that Bethel wouldn't grow many crops; the soil was especially bad for garden vegetables some of the women said. So, I wasn't surprised when most people thought their new marshal should stick to pistols and prisoners instead of pickles and potatoes that first year in Bethel. I went to the edge of town, selected a small hillside no one claimed and cleared the surface brush. I dug the soil and it felt rich and firm in my hand, so much so, I cleared a spot 100' x 75'. Near the garden I dug a root cellar into the hillside. The temperature in the cellar stayed a constant 38 degrees until the spring sun began to drive the cold into the ground, then I needed a little additional heat to prevent freezing. After several years of proving my point, the N.C. Company ran electricity to the location for me. Then, when the cold began to penetrate in February, I would turn on a single light bulb which maintained the warmth needed in the cellar to prevent freezing until spring breakup arrived.

Encouraged by the success of the garden and root cellar operation, I set about to build a greenhouse that would enable me to produce more food and start some crops that would not mature in the normally short Alaskan summer.

The greenhouse was 24' x 12' with the back wall built solid and filled with 10" of sawdust insulation. The roof was 10' high in the back and sloped toward the front. The south sloping roof caught the full rays of the early spring sun and answered many of my growing problems in the new garden operation. I would soak beans until they sprouted, then plant the sprouts in the greenhouse, later to be transplanted outside. I grew abundant harvests of greenbeans. The Bethel prisoners ate a lot of greenbeans and potatoes in the 1940's, for if there were two things I could grow, it was beans and potatoes.

The only fresh vegetables during the winter months were those stored in the root cellars of the townspeople. Part of my popularity may have been that I always had sufficient vegetables to give away.

Blueberries were abundant on the brushy tundra. Usually it became a village project as each household gathered berries for jelly and jam, as well as storage for the long winter.

To speed the process of cleaning the berries for storage, a trough about 10 feet long was built of wood and lined with gunny sack, or old wool blanket. The berries were always picked on dry sunny days to insure they had no moisture on them. Each container was emptied into the slightly elevated end of the trough. As the berries rolled slowly down the trough the leaves and trash would stick to the blanket lining, producing only clean blueberries at the mouth.

Butter usually arrived in Bethel in 50 pound kegs of brine water. The kegs were treasured possessions and saved judiciously by every family as containers for food storage. Each householder counted the kegs in the root cellar and took great comfort in knowing his winter cache contained, among other things, several kegs of blueberries and salted salmon berries. A rule of thumb was: fill your cellar and have $400 if you want to live through the winter.

There were thousands of ptarmigan nesting in the tundra each spring outside of Bethel. They reared their young in the brushy undercover until they could fly, then, as fall approached, the young joined the adult birds in flocks "as thick as grasshoppers."

In the evening they migrated to an area across the Kuskokwim, back of the Army base, to roost for the night. There, in the big willows and alders on an island, they seemed to find a sense of security. In the early morning hours the daily migration began back across the river to the seeds and berries in the flats above Bethel. I often have timed their flight to take over an hour for the daily migration, which would be repeated in reverse in the evening. Often, while using a shotgun I have dropped several birds with one shot. The breast of ptarmigan is a succulent delicacy for the most discriminating taste. My prisoners often requested ptarmigan for Sunday dinner; I had no difficulty in fulfilling their wish.

Ducks and geese were in abundance in the delta country and everyone's winter meat contained an abundant supply. There was much wildlife wasted in those early years in Bethel. The local population of the villages would make drives on the lakes with their canoes in the summertime when the ducks and geese were moulting and couldn't fly. The canoes on the lakes would drive the birds onto the bank where the waiting men, women and children would kill them with clubs. A visit to any of the villages would indicate they had taken far more than they could use; the piles of dead geese and duck were often spoiling.

I would talk to them and explain how everyone needed to help in preserving the animals and birds if they were to remain abundant. Soon after I became a one-man conservationist, the Fish and Wildlife department sent two men to the Bethel area, Jim Cragg and Roy Woodruff, to help enforce the trapping and game laws.

Cragg was a tough wildlife man, but fair and honest with the people he sought to help. He had once been a cowboy in a rodeo and had led something of a vagabond's life. He and I had much in common and became close friends. Many illegal trappers and hunters can remember a pair of lawmen who, with what seemed uncanny ability, appeared at the right place and the wrong time for the violators. After several years, the impact of education, compassion and enforcement began to change the wasteful habits of the rural inhabitants of the delta country.

Enforcement sometimes produced embarassment when the past caught up with me. In the late 1930's and early 1940's, the sparse populations made game laws difficult to enforce, and the very fact of the small number of inhabitants helped to preserve the wildlife. Most people looked the other way unless there was flagrant misuse of the game.

As an avid hunter, and many think an excellent cook, I invited Jim Cragg, Roy Woodruff and Ethyl Peasgood to my cabin in Bethel to share in the benefits of a recent goose hunt. I had prepared roast goose and all the trimmings available to make it a feast.

As we sat enjoying what the others called "excellent cuisine", Ethyl remarked, "Oh this goose is good, but you know the best goose I ever ate in my life was up at Takotna. Ted, do you remember that old native that came down the river in the spring and brought geese into town and sold them. You bought one from him and roasted it."

My face began to turn red as the two wildlife men looked at each other with sly grins. Several times I tried to interrupt her recounting the event, since springtime is never a legal time to hunt geese. I tried to explain that was when I first went to Takotna and meat was in low supply, but the two wildlife men weren't about to let me off so easy. Until Jim Cragg died he always kidded me about eating illegal goose.

One of my legal goose hunts almost cost me my life; in fact, it was one of the geese being served at the table the night of my embarrassment.

Many calls to the villages afforded me extra moments to fish and hunt after the incident was cleared for which I had been called. Such a call had taken me down to the Bering Sea at the mouth of the Kuskokwim. I had never shot snow geese before, and word had been passed along that the snow geese were thick in the mud flats near Kwigillingok. Goose season was open, so I packed my shotgun into the plane that was to fly me to the native village.

Hiring a native and his boat to take me up one of the sloughs about 12 miles, I pitched my tent on the flats where the geese had been feeding and bedding down when the tide ran them off the mud flats; the native left with instructions to return the next day and get me.

I shot a lot of geese the first day and intended to be out on the flats before daybreak to get the rest of my winter meat supply. The night was miserably cold and I slept very little. In the early hours after midnight I fell asleep and didn't awaken until the sun was well up in the sky. As I crawled from my pup tent, I scanned the sky for some sign of geese. Far in the distance, over the mudflats, I could see thousands of them, but none near my tent. Finishing a hurried breakfast, I pulled on my hipboots and started for the flats nearer the salt water. The tide was out and the tidal flats formed a broad, muddy expanse to the horizon.

Walking along with my shotgun ready, I didn't notice the change in the surface of the flats until the bottom gave way and I was over my knees in mud. Each movement to free myself only sucked me deeper into the mire. Within minutes I had sunk to the top of my boots. I could see the salt water and realized the tide was coming in. Visions of being unable to free myself and the tidal water covering me caused me to struggle to pull my feet from the boots—that effort only worked me deeper and the pressure was too great to get free, besides my boots were tied below my knees. Panic is man's worst enemy in difficult situations, and I knew this. I stopped to evaluate the circumstances and prayed. Removing my raincoat, I carefully placed my shotgun on top of it. Then, laying back on the mud to remove my weight from my feet, and provide a broader base, I slowly began to pull one boot out of the mire. At first nothing happened, then I realized my right leg was higher than my left and I knew I was going to get free before the tide covered me.

By the time both legs were free the tidal water was nearly to my raincoat. The geese were filling the sky in a blanket of white as I moved quickly back to a positon of safety. The water was about 12 inches deep where I decided to squat low and wait for the geese to fly straight instead of veering from my movement on the mud flat. From the squatting position I fired and knocked down two large snow geese that fell almost at my feet. The second shot came while I was slightly off balance and kicked me over backwards into the water, filling my boots and soaking the remainder of my dry clothing. That seemed enough for one day; I picked up my geese and headed for the relative safety of my canvas tent and a warm campfire.

The native man didn't show up that evening as he had promised and the night chill settled on the flats. I shivered in the early darkness. Nothing seemed to warm me and I spent the night feeling more ready to freeze to death than survive. There was not enough wood on the tundra flats to build much fire and my wet clothing never dried. I wished the night through that I had brought my sleeping bag—at least I could have gotten warm.

The next morning the boat came to pick me up and we went to Kwilgillingok. I hired some native women to clean my kill because they would not leave even the fuzz on them. They always picked the heads clean too since the heads were a delicacy to them. I stayed with the missionaries in Kwigillingok that night flew back to Bethel with my geese as my only prisoners. Storing them in the N.C. Company freezer, I felt my winter meat of goose was secure.

Goose hunting seemed to be the one sport that haunted me with unexpected circumstances everytime I went. The experience was no different when the Alaska Native Service officer, Ron Bailey, visited Bethel and invited me to go hunting with him.

The red Cessena hit heavy turbulence shortly after take-off from the Kuskokwim river at Bethel. Flying westward toward the salt flats we commented that wind like we were in sure would keep the geese on the ground, and if the fowl didn't fly in that kind of weather, perhaps we shouldn't either.

The pilot approached the inlet heading straight into the wind. As we skimmed the choppy surface, he eased back on the throttle and allowed the little plane to settle onto the waves that seemed far bigger after the plane was floating. Taxiing to the bank, the float scraped into the soft mud and seemed secure. The pilot opened the door, climbed onto the float, and ran to the front of the plane before I could gather my gear stowed in the rear seat. When he jumped from the float, the lightened aircraft floated and the strong wind blew us into the open water. Waves in the inlet were large enough to swamp the plane. If the plane should survive to reach the far side without power it would be smashed on the rocks that lined the shore.

I had never piloted an airplane nor had any lessons, but I had flown in the right hand seat with expert pilots and observed the many controls and instruments with interest. With the calm assurance that seemed easy for me when I was in tight situations, I turned the key and hit the starter. The warm engine responded immediately and I eased the throttle forward slowly; the plane began to respond and pull against the driving wind toward the startled pilot on shore.

The pilot began to shout, wave his arms and run up and down the bank. I wondered if he was trying to get out of my way or tell me something as I gently worked the rudder peddles and eased the plane upon the mud just as the engine died. Only the gas left in the carberator had saved me, the plane—and maybe the pilot on shore in front of me.

Climbing from the aircraft to throw the tie rope to the pilot, I was honestly surprised by the response of my hunting friend. It was years later before I realized that most men don't taxi float planes solo without hours of instructions. The incident brought an end to my career as a pilot; the load of white geese only enhanced the story when we got back, as the pilot told how I had saved his plane from certain disaster.

Fish have always played an important part in the food supply of Alaskans and the variety of fish can vary the diet to most anyone's taste. My prisoners always wanted as many different kind as I could catch.

In the early summer, just before the king salmon start to run—usually right after breakup—the smelt start their migration up the rivers. The Kuskokwim is noted for its heavy run of smelt.

The smelt is a small fish about 10 inches long that is best fried. Villagers would go to the river during the smelt run with their dip nets, which sometimes surfaced so full they couldn't be lifted from the water. The first fish resulted in a big fish fry on the banks and smelt feeds were a true sign that winter was gone for awhile. After the first catches, the rest were hung to dry in the warm sun.

As the smelt run began tapering off, king salmon would begin their migration back to the waters of their birth to spawn. Netting was legal then and everyone put their nets in the water. Sometimes a net would catch as many as 30 big kings; nets were always run twice a day.

Kings were usually smoked instead of dried. A large building, about two stories tall, would be constructed. A ditch sloping from the building would be dug to a pit about fifteen feet away. The trench was then covered with sticks and dirt and a fire built in the pit to produce smoke that was sucked through a chimney draft into the smokehouse. Inside the smokehouse, pole racks would hold row upon row of salmon strips. Smoke from the smoldering alder would penetrate the fish to form a succulent meat for winter. One summer I smoked 400 pounds of salmon strips, salted six kegs of salmon bellies and canned 300 #2 cans of salmon. The prisoners in the Bethel jail always ate well.

Work can be play if the mood is right. Jim Cragg and I were called above the village of Aniak to investigate reports of illegal beaver trapping and trade of illegal pelts. Summer was in full swing and the silver salmon were running in the river. After our legal business was done, we flew to a point about 20 miles from Aniak where a fresh, clear steam flows into the Kuskokwim. We anchored our float plane and watched the water boil with silvers running in the eddy formed by an incoming stream. Scrambling to get our poles, both of us ran along the bank until we were sure we each stood at exactly the right spot. Both of us cast simultaneously and our daredevil lures had barely touched the water when salmon hit both of them. We fought our fish to the bank and repeated the performance.

I had some prisoners to deliver to Fairbanks from the Bethel jail, and it was an accepted fact that I bring some of the game from Bethel as gifts to those less fortunate in the structured city life of Fairbanks.

Sometimes it is difficult for a fisherman to know when he has gotten tired or caught all the fish he can carry. When Jim and I gathered our catches, Jim realized the load was too heavy for the plane to carry. At first the solution seemed to lay in Jim making several trips alone to carry the fish. But in the baggage compartment of the plane, we found some canvas bags. So we filled each bag with fish, tied them onto the floats of the plane, and taxied the 20 miles down river to Aniak.

The strange sight of a plane coming down river with water rippling white around the floats indicated trouble. By the time we reached the docks a crowd had gathered. I suppose everyone admires a good fish story—especially if you have the fish to go with it. Several of the silvers were quite large, and the village of Aniak was having a contest for the biggest salmon caught during the silver run. Jim had caught the biggest one, though mine was almost as large. So with due fisherman pride, Jim marched off to the N.C. Store to weigh his catch; the village of Aniak followed.

As I continued to unload the fish an idea came to me. Taking the biggest silver from my group I began poking tiny rocks and pebbles in the salmon's mouth. With a small stick I foced the rocks into the bell until I filled the silver with them, then I headed for the N.C. Store.

"Well, Jim, your fish is big but I have never seen a salmon as heavy as this one I caught. It's sure a heavy one and we ought to weigh it," I chided. Jim didn't mind; his was the biggest silver every caught in Aniak, and he knew it.

I hoisted my silver onto the scales, and it went over the weight of Jim's salmon by 1¼ pounds. Everybody stood amazed. Some began mumbling about how much shorter my fish was in spite of its great weight. However, when I picked the fish up from the scales I got him by the tail instead of the mouth and rocks scattered everywhere. The mob chased me back to the docks with Jim in the lead. Jim got the prize even though my joke almost backfired before I could convince the mob that it was just against my friend, who really had caught the biggest fish.

CHAPTER X

DEATH STALKS THE BUSHDWELLER

Drunks, fights, shootings and rape were not all of life in Bethel—though it was often a big part of it. Sometimes, the problems I faced were the result of the domestic life the village lived.

In an Alaska village of the 1940's, dog teams were as much a part of life as was the automobile to the more mechanized world. The new machine had not yet made its dubious impact on my wilderness world as a faster means of transportation; the dog to Alaskans was revered much as the cowboy's horse in earlier America. The dog team could save a man's life on the winter trail, sometimes as transportaion, sometimes by putting all the dogs in the shelter with him and warming by their body heat. The dog is still trusted by many Alaskans as the best companion a person can have.

This concept of the importance of a canine animal in the life-stream of the arctic enhanced my problems of trying to marshal in a village community that often had more population than the legal census figure, with everyone's relatives living in town when hunting or fishing was not necessary.

In the summertime, the residents of Bethel would turn their dogs loose to roam as they willed. This saved on feeding them as well as allowed cross-breeding of the animals. In the fall, when the pups were getting large enough to show their best characteristics, the owner would pick out his team and discard the rest. The problem arose because there was not enough food for the hungry animals; garbage was problem enough without help from the dogs.

Complaints often came to me that someone had been bitten by a stray dog, or that some child had been chased home by an overzealous animal. I would appeal to the people each time to tie up their dogs, but few responded and the problem increased. Whenever people congregated, arguments on the dog question were sure to erupt. I had become unreasonable some said, this request was out of the question others argued.

One summer day a small native boy was walking down a side street in Bethel, oblivious to anything other than the rock he was hitting with a willow stick. A pack of dogs, led by a bitch in heat, broke out of the brush near the boy and ran toward him. No one knows for sure what happened after that, except the child was attacked by the dogs. A neighbor, hearing the cries of the boy rushed into the street screaming; the dogs ran back into the bush.

The bloody, mangled body of the little boy lay motionless on the ground. The hysterical screams of the woman brought other neighbors; someone picked up the child and rushed him to the hospital. The child opened his eyes once when the truck hit a bump, but when the doctor listened with his stethoscope for the tiny heartbeat, there was none.

Bethel seemed strangely silent that night. I should have done something about those dogs long ago, some said; all knew I had tried many times before.

The N.C. Co. showed a movie several nights each week in a building that served as the Bethel Theatre. Announcements and advertisements of local business people were flashed on the screen prior to the feature film. No one was surprised at the first slide to appear on the night following the death of the little boy: ALL DOGS MUST BE TIED, AND REMAIN TIED AT ALL TIMES. AFTER FOUR DAYS, ANY DOG RUNNING LOOSE ON THE STREET WILL BE SHOT. BY ORDER OF THE U.S. MARSHAL. I decided we had already waited too long.

This time there was no argument. The stunned population went about their task, enforced by the grim reminder of a child's death. On the morning of the fifth day, I loaded my rifle shortly after breakfast and began to patrol the streets and alleys of Bethel. I shot twenty-five dogs that first day, but now the town was behind me and no one argued if they saw their dog thrown on the truck. Five years and one life had gone into the enforcement of a simple order, but the secret lay in the people understanding the justice behind the order. This attitude of "bush justice" often was the secret of any success I had as marshal when I went into remote villages. I believed people basically wanted law and order, and it was much easier to enforce what the majority wanted.

There is something about doing your best as a Marshal that soothes the tragedy of misguided youth, or the reckless living of adults, when my badge became a symbol to both. There were the helpless moments of life when no amount of help was adequate, yet as a Marshal I was called to do what I could. Such a time as this is still vivid in my memory.

The day was peaceful and the mosquitoes were finished in early fall; it was a perfect day to just sit outside the cabin door and watch the fluffy white clouds bellowing above the September thunderheads to the south. I felt at peace just to be alive on a warm sunny day in Bethel. I was sitting, during one of the few quiet moments I could call my own, in front of the log jail near the river.

"Marshal, Marshal," the shouts jarred me from my daydreaming. "Come quick Marshal, Dull tipped his canoe over in honey bucket slough and hasn't come back up."

Honey bucket slough! The thought of it was enough to sicken me. Back of the Bethel Roadhouse was a pothole lake with no outlet or inlet. It was a hundred yards in diameter and very deep. With no public sewage system, the townspeople used the lake to dump their toilet buckets, called honeypots; the odor from the pit should have been enough to keep the boys away. In this instance, they had put in a canoe and were hunting ducks that landed on the slough. The lake had been used for years as the honey pit for all of Bethel; when the summer wind shifted, the fragrance was a telltale sign from which direction it came. I was reminded of these things as we ran toward the honey pit; it seemed strange that such thoughts would come when tragedy was probably in the making.

On the way to the slough, the story from the frightened youth became more coherent; the boys had shot a duck and the Dull boy had gone after it in his canoe and overturned. The duck was about 50 feet from shore. As we ran to the pit, I spotted the canoe floating upside down, just as the boy had said. Shore ice had formed a few feet out from the bank; I noticed this too; the water would be cold.

113

A picture flashed into my mind that had haunted me for years. When I was five, my Grandfather had given a new fishing pole to my brother, Jimmy, and me. We lived in Echo, Oregon, near the Umatilla River. We wanted to go fishing, but my mother wouldn't let us even though my brother was eight. One day we took the fishing pole and went without permission. Just below our house, the railroad crossed the river. We climbed onto the bridge and were fishing a deep hole in the river below the bridge when Jimmy climbed onto the truss rods along the bridge and fell into the river. He had always bragged to me that he could swim, so I began to call to him to swim out. He would just come to the surface and look at me with a horrified expression and go down again without making a sound.

Thinking like a five-year-old, I ran to get my cousin who lived nearby and was a good swimmer. At the end of the railroad bridge I met a man and excitedly told him what was happening. He assured me he would save my brother, and we ran to the bank of the river. Jimmy was still splashing in the water as the man sat down to remove his shoes. He had his laces untied when Jimmy surfaced again. The man tied his shoes back on and said, "I don't think I can get him out," and walked away. Jimmy was about ten feet from shore and I watched as he went under for the last time.

The scene could have been the same to me as I ran along the bank of honey bucket slough. Without hesitation, I jumped into the honey pit, swam to the canoe and dived into the muck. Opening my eyes near the surface, I had to close them before I went very deep because of the sediment and slime. Again and again I dived into the thick refuse until, exhausted, I barely swam to shore. In the the urgency of the moment, I had jumped in with my glasses on and had lost them. When I reached the bank, I sent the boy who had summoned me to spread the alarm to the village. Moments later some older boys came with a boat and began to drag the honey pit. I could do no more and walked back to my cabin to clean up. I thought about the man who could have saved my brother from drowning in the Umatilla River and wondered if he had done his best that day; at least I had tried.

Dropping my clothes at the door, I prepared a bath, first with soap and then with clorox water in an attempt to remove the smell. Scrubbing from head to foot helped, but the smell lingered for days on my body. After cleaning myself and getting dressed, I returned to the slough. They found the lifeless body as I arrived.

Life is measured in minutes in the icy waters of Alaska, much less the cold sewage water of honey bucket slough. Most Eskimos never learn to swim because of the low temperature of water even in the warmest part of summer. Every year that I was Marshal on the Kuskokwim, somebody drowned in the river or lakes, because they could not swim. Death by drowning was a accepted fact, though never taken lightly.

Weeks after the Dull boy drowned in the honey pit, a knock on the door brought me to my feet as Mr. Dull walked into the Marshal's office. In his hand he carried a small package he had received in the mail and handed it to me.

As I opened the package, the man turned and opened the door. With the door half-opened, he looked back at me and said, "It isn't much of a way to say thanks for trying, Marshal, but the wife and I want you to know we appreciate what you did for our boy."

Inside the cardboard box was a new pair of glasses, ground to my prescription, and almost a duplicate of the ones I lost in the honey pit.

Sadness lasts forever when lives are bound together by relationships and dependence upon each other. Although a person may not compliment the community, sadness results if the life ends in a tragic manner.

Mail arrived in Bethel by dogteam in the winter on a regular run from Oscarville to Bethel. The carrier was a hard-drinking oldtimer who seemed to always be more drunk than sober, and one who never feared, or cared about the dangerous cold of winter. He always made it through with the mail, not always on time, but always coming through between the two villages.

Leaving Oscarville, after drinking all day, he headed for Bethel. A strong dog team with a good lead dog can pull a load of about 100 pounds per dog without too much difficulty. The mail load was light and the drunk carrier decided to ride. The dogs made good speed along the well-traveled trail until they neared Bethel. Using the river as a great white highway, the dogs held a steady pace under the full moon that reflected the points of a million shiney spots in the glistening snow. The warmth of a robe cover and the movement of the sled soon brought sleep to the over-indulgent mail carrier.

Nearing Bethel, the lead dog turned toward the lights of the village and quickened the pace. Thin ice covered a portion of water near the bank, which held the weight of the lead dog but gave way under the weight of the sled. When the sled dropped below the surface, it pulled the wheel dogs in with it, dumping the mail and passenger under the ice. The trained instinct of the lead dog caused him to lean into his harness with extra strength, pulling the other dogs out of the water. The sled remained in the hole and held them anchored near death. No one knows how long this struggle continued before the scene was noticed by a passing musher. The thin ice was over an eddy that had no current or the dogs would have been dragged under the ice and lost. Summoning help from the village, the passing musher and village men pulled the sled ashore and released the team. All of the mail was lost, but their grappling hooks soon snagged the body of the carrier and pulled him to the surface from the shallow water. Death stands close to life whenever travelers cross arctic waste and challenge elements which show no mercy.

The Bering Sea, at the mouth of the Kuskokwim, was colder than water up river, which caused flooding of some sort almost annually. The river ice breaks up at the headwaters and starts flowing toward the mouth. Ice jams form huge frozen dams and can bring destruction to villages along the river bank. One year McGrath flooded so badly, I tied my boat to the second story railing of the McGrath Roadhouse and entered the building from the second floor.

The worst disaster in Bethel came in 1948. The lower Kuskokwim was frozen hard when the upper river began to flow. The freezing temperature in the Bay refused to allow the pressure of the moving ice to break its hold on the river. I remember the townspeople of Bethel standing on the banks in mute silence as the obvious came closer to reality. The water began to back up behind the ice dam and soon the deep river banks had disappeared.

The flat delta country offers some salvation for its residents when rivers flood. Once they go over the banks, there are thousands of square miles for the flooding water to expand. The inhabitants of Bethel moved to higher ground outside of town and camped for five days until the water subsided. The material damage was staggering; the town had an average of two feet of water flowing through it and spots where the water was six feet deep. Mud and debris filled most homes, but on the high ground a carnival atmosphere existed. During the five days, motorboats traveled to the houses to gather needed supplies. My log jail only had two prisoners at the time of the flood. They became a part of the crew assigned to move personal affects to higher ground. When the water finally subsided, no lives had been lost, for which the town was grateful.

Everyone in a bush family must carry an equal share of responsibility for the family's continued survival and in meeting everyday needs.

116

Even children join parents in what would otherwise be considered adult tasks. On one of my visits to the coast, some men told me this story:

Numaiyuk, a nine-year-old boy of Kwigillingok, left the village in early moring to gather firewood. The day was bright and the dogs seemed playful as they easily pulled the weight of the boy and the empty sled. Farther and farther they ran, the sharp eyes of the youth, accustomed to watching for dead wood, sweeping the horizon of the flat marsh lands inland from Kwigillingok.

The noon sun hung low on the edge of the earth as he stopped his half-loaded sled, fed his dogs some dried fish and sat down to eat his portion. The clouds to the southwest formed a black contrast to the white waste of the land around him. He knew their meaning; a storm would soon sweep in from the Bering Sea. He must leave to reach home before that happened, but the sled was not full and his family was short of wood. He chose to look for a few more minutes then head back.

Minutes stretched into an hour. He did not think of the storm again until the angry clouds swallowed the sun's brightness. The he turned the dogs for home. Within an hour the wind began to blow and light snow stung his face; the dogs raced on, seeming to sense the urgency in their young driver's yells.

Darkness came early in the gathering storm. By midafternoon the full blast of a Bering Sea blizzard made travel impossible.

In Kwigillingok, a worried mother walked to the door of her sod igloo and felt the freezing blast of the icy winds. The driving snow spun through the door and chilled the tiny room. If her son were but a man, he would know what to do, she thought as she closed the door and turned to get her parka.

At her neighbor's igloo she spoke briefly with the woman and then turned back into the storm. House to house she went, asking the neighbors to pray that God would keep young Numaiyuk safe from the storm. Soon the entire village gathered together to pray for the safety of the boy who was caught in the vicious blizzard.

All through the night they prayed. The storm did not abate until morning. As the calm returned to Kwigillingok, the people who lived with the likelihood of death arose from the seated circle of friends to go to their own igloo. No one spoke; everyone knew the chance Numaiyuk had for survival alone on the trail.

When the boy realized the storm was too strong to travel into, he called his dogs to stop. Taking a stick from the sled, he began to dig furiously in the snow. The wind made the loose snow swirl into his face, but his frantic digging soon made a hole six feet in diameter and four feet deep. Unhitching his dog team, Numaiyuk brought the five dogs into the hole with him. He slipped his lead dog inside his coat and closed the fur around them. Through the night the five dogs seemed to sense the danger they were in with Numaiyuk. The chill factor was near fifty below outside; huddled together under a drift of snow the boy and dogs lay still and quiet—comfortable by comparison to their alternative in the wind. Soon, all of them slept.

Numaiyuk could not hear the howl of the storm when he awoke. Thinking at first he was dead, he refused to move. Then, one of the dogs pushed out of the snowbank; the quiet world of white emptiness lay silent in the sun. Numaiyuk became a nine-year-old again and danced around the sled with each dog jumping to play with him. He gave each dog one fish and ate one himself. The trip home on the wind-packed snow was fun. The runners of the sled seemed to fly over the snow.

"Mother," he said rushing through the door, "I didn't find much wood, there was a storm."

The grateful mother pulled Numaiyuk to her breast and said over and over, "Thank God, thank God."

The village of Kwigillingok believed more in God that day than any mother could remember. Numaiyuk had proved he could be a man in a hostile wilderness with God's help and a mother's prayer.

CHAPTER XI

HONEST ESKIMO

Tundra villages, scattered along rivers and lakes of the delta country, were served by me as the marshal from Bethel. If the village had a law enforcement problem they called my office in Bethel. I would then go to the assistance of the village in whatever way was necessary

The villages were well organized with a village council and chief. The organization was the kind needed and desired by those using it, though not necessarily the kind of organization desired by the white men who considered their customs primitive. When a crime was committed in the village, the council would first summon me. When I arrived in the village, even though I had a warrant for an individual's arrest, I would go first to the village council and let them sign a complaint and ask their feelings on the matter. They knew what they wanted done and without exception they demanded harder punishment than would have been given otherwise. The villages were pretty much their own law, with me serving as their agency of enforcement.

I spent many hours, trying to be as patient as the Eskimos I was working with, telling the village leaders that when someone does wrong they must pay for it. When I made an arrest the same ritual was

119

performed again for the prisoner. They knew the bush justice of the Kuskokwim Marshal was fair and seemed to respect me for it. If my logic could convince them of their wrong action then they usually went along willingly.

As in other societies there were felonies, robberies and rapes. Those offenders usually went to the Federal Penitentiary on McNeil Island; but the bush Eskimos were no worse than whites in this respect.

Most of the people were honest; many minor offenses were taken before the U.S. Commissioner's court in Bethel. The offenders then served their jail sentences in my log jail. In the more serious cases, the U.S. Commissioner would bind them over to the Grand Jury in Fairbanks, and it became my job to transport my prisoner safely to the Fairbanks jail. They were then tried in the United States District Court and sentenced.

The honesty of the natives, and the trust earned by me, made my job of being the only lawman in the delta possible to perform. The truth was not difficult to find if I asked in the villages. I was trusted and the natives were honest—together it became a winning combination.

The spring flood of 1948 caught the Army as unprepared as it had the residents of Bethel. The storage of over 100 drums of stove oil near the slough behind the Post left oil drums scattered in the brush on a small island and along the river bank. Delay by the army is not procrastination, they are just slow getting the job done. The oil drums remained in the brush during the summer and early fall, and may have remained much longer had someone not discovered they had been taken.

A custom among the Eskimos in Alaska embraces a communal concept that is born of sharing one's possessions and the need of another. If an Eskimo has a need, and you have something you aren't using that will fill that need, it is not stealing from him to take it and use it. The army had difficulty appreciating this custom when they discovered their oil drums missing, not that it would have made any difference had they known who took them.

The Commander called me to report the stolen oil and demanded that I do something about it.

I turned my boat into the backwater of the slough behind the Army base as eased back on the throttle. I was looking for anything to indicate what had happened but it didn't take training to see that someone, or some group, had cut paths in the alders and rolled the drums to the water's edge. Close inspection indicated they had loaded the drums into boats and carried them away by the river.

Pulling pack into the current of the Kuskokwim, I opened the throttle of the ten horse Johnson outboard and headed down stream. At Oscarville, the first village below Bethel, I tied my boat to a log near the bank as I talked with the a group of boys. Questioning the village men, I began to put the story together. They hadn't really thought they were stealing the oil. Yes, they had taken the oil that was abandoned, and so had men all along the river. Taking their statements, I went to other villages and the story was repeated. When the names were made known, I recorded them, then headed for the next village.

After ten individual's signed statements, though there had been more than one hundred barrels cached when the flood hit, I turned my boat back towards Bethel.

Before the U.S. Commissioner, I swore complaints against the ten men because the Army was demanding that the federal matter be cleared. The oil was federal property and something had to be done. The situation was getting sticky and I was caught in the middle. Since the matter was "federal" I decided one way to satisfy everyone would be to call in the FBI. I called the Anchorage office and they immediately sent a man to accompany me. The army felt sure justice would be done now that an FBI man was in company of the U.S. Marshal.

The FBI agent was a congenial fellow with an understanding way. He could see that it wasn't a planned "ripoff" of military property and was reluctant to perform his task with me. We were two men with orders we did not like. As we slowed our boat and pulled into Oscarville, the propeller hit a floating tree limb. We were still forty yards from shore. The tide was in and the river's current had almost ceased. When the propeller hit the log it sheared a pin in the prop and we stopped immediately. I always carried extra pins and it was just a matter of putting in a new one.

I found it easier to tilt the motor and reach for the propeller than to take the motor off and into the boat. I carefully unscrewed the nut and removed the propeller. After slipping in the new pin I reached to put the propeller in place, but dropped it into the river. Grabbing a long pike pole I carried in the boat I shoved it into the muddy bottom and threw the anchor overboard. The crowd on the bank watched as the two of us sat helplessly looking at each other for answers. The water was murky and the bottom muddy. The nearest prop blade was on the bottom of the river; the next nearest was probably in Bethel, or

Anchorage.

The FBI agent slowly got to his feet and began to pull off his clothes and shoes. He stripped to his skin. Women and children on the bank were coming alive with excitement as each garment fell to the bottom of the boat. Clad in nothing but his birthday suit, the agent dove into the cold river. This added more noise on the riverbank because most Eskimos can't swim. They are fearful of the icy water and avoid ever going into the river if possible. On the third dive the agent stayed under longer than usual. I was getting anxious when the grinning face and uplifted arm broke water with the lost propeller held high in the air. While I repaired the motor the shivering agent dressed to the cheers of the crowd that had observed a most unusual sight.

Tying the boat to the same log I had used before, I discovered everyone wanted to talk about the skinny-dipper more than about the reason for our visit. Locating the men whose names I had taken earlier, I served the warrants and told them they would have to come along. They willingly climbed into my boat as we continued downstream to the other villages.

Soon the boat was loaded and I made arrangements to hire a second boat. One of the arrested native men volunteered to take his own boat. When all ten warrants were served, three boats headed back to Bethel. The ten "arrested" men were in two boats preceding me and the FBI agent in the third.

In a holiday mood, the ten arrested men docked their boats and went before the U.S. Commissioner with me and the agent. Justice is best served when it requires the least amount of enforcing. The Commissioner offered to turn the ten men loose if they would pay for the oil they had. They were given suspended sentences, since none had any money, and released. They left the village as happy as they had arrived. Evey man eventually paid the amount assessed him for the oil he said he had taken, without any pressure from me. The natives learned, too, that they shouldn't touch government material even if it looked abandoned, unless it had been declared abandoned.

The Eskimo of the delta would do what was expected of him by law—if he knew the law. Sometimes his ignorance of the law made his honesty more demanding when the law became known.

During World War II, the Japanese had an ingenious idea. It didn't work very well, but the idea was a good one. They would release gas-filled balloons into the prevailing winds which would carry the balloons over the Pacific Northwest. Attached to each balloon was an incendiary bomb. The bomb was designed to detonate upon impact and was intended for the forests of the Northwest. The winds were not always predictable and many of the fire bombs landed in western Alaska.

Orders were issued by the Military that all unexploded bombs discovered by the inhabitants of western Alaska were to be reported to the Military, or U.S. Marshal's office, immediately. Many of the bombs did not detonate when they hit the soft tundra and marsh areas of the delta country and became hazards to inhabitants. I passed word to individuals and the radio continued to warn citizens of the danger.

In a remote village down the Kuskokwim river below Oscarville, lived a lone native trapper who seldom heard a radio. He was remotely aware that a war was on, but it didn't touch his village or disrupt his trapline, consequently it meant little to him.

One day he checked his mink traps and headed toward the hill country above Aniak village. The sun was bright and his dogs were running well; they knew the trapline as well as the man who controlled them. Breaking out of the brush into an open area near a small lake, the trapper noticed a strange object almost in the middle of the clearing. As the dogs approached, the wind caused the balloon to swing in their direction and they bolted out of the trail. The trapper got them under control and turned his sled on its side to prevent a runaway by the team. He walked cautiously toward the thing that had frightened his dogs; he soon realized it was mechanical and apparently something someone had lost. After careful examination, he disconnected the device with the strange markings and carried it to his sled. He was twenty-five miles from his village, but all the way home he imagined the excitement, and the attention he would get when they saw the strange find he had among the dead beaver and mink in his sled.

There was still much daylight as he neared the village. His dogs began to yelp in response to other teams staked near houses he passed. Stopping in front of the village trading post, he called to friends to come see what he had trapped that day. The smiling trapper was struck dumb as the crowd he had gathered began to mumble and disperse rapidly. Calling each by name until someone stopped running, he inquired as to why they all acted so strangely.

"The Marshal has been on radio about those things. We are not suppose to touch. They are dangerous. Army say leave them alone and call them or the Marshal," the friend said before fleeing.

The native trapper turned his team around, after having just completed a trip of fifty miles, and headed back along the trail. The bouncing incendiary was cradled among the dead, trapped animals and didn't explode. Darkness had long since prevailed when the team stopped. Carefully removing his strange cargo, he placed the bomb in exactly the same cradle of snow he had found it.

When he reached home again he proudly notified me at Bethel that he had found a bomb. He offered his apologies for having disturbed the bomb—he didn't know it was wrong at the time—but I could find the bomb exactly where it had fallen, twenty-five dog-sled miles into the bush.

I never ceased to marvel at the simple honesty of the native people. I did notice that the more they were around white people the easier it was for them to be untruthful. I was fortunate to be their Marshal before they learned much about the "white man's ways."

CHAPTER XII

BUSH JUSTICE

"Marshal, Aniak radio just contacted the schoolteacher and they want you to come up there—there's been a shooting," the native boy said to me as he stood in the doorway of the log jailhouse.

"Okay, son, and thanks for coming over. Here, this dime will only buy ice cream," I replied, as I pitched the coin in the air for him to catch. His grin spread from ear to ear as he ran out the door.

Aniak was a village about eighty land miles from Bethel, and more than twice that distance by boat. I decided to charter a plane; I could arrive in forty-five minutes and get back the same day if things went well.

The U.S. Commissioner in Aniak, Mrs. Wilson, was also the postmistress. She had moved into town from a gold claim on Marvel Creek when her husband died and now held two prominent positions in the Aniak community.

I went to see her first and got what little information she had. She told me the man was a big fellow, smart, and mean when he was drinking—which was most of the time. His cabin was across the river and the native people nearby had turned in the report that he had shot his wife.

"Sorry, Ted, that's all I know," she said with a sigh, "but you be careful, I hear he's a mean one."

The cabin, made of logs and set well back into the trees, would have been idyllic under different conditions. I approached slowly and as naturally as possible; if the man was inside I sure didn't want to confront the same 30-06 that had taken the woman's life. Stepping to one side, I rapped hard on the rough board door. The hole and splintered wood confirmed part of the story; the man had shot her, supposedly, through the door with the bullet hitting her in the back of the head.

From inside the cabin I could hear a thick-tongued response to each knock. Easing the door open, I saw a big man sitting at the only table in the room with a glass in his hand.

"I'm the U.S. Marshal. I hear there's been some trouble over here." I said.

The man offered me a chair and began to tell his story. He had made a keg of homebrew and was drinking heavily. The more he drank the meaner he got which in turn made him want to drink more. The man, admittedly, was known as a trouble-maker and tried to live up to his reputation. His wife tried to leave because he was becoming violent. He had grabbed her and jerked her back into the house several times. The last time he locked the door so she couldn't leave. He then loaded his rifle and told her he would blow a nasty hole in her head with the 30-06 if she tried to escape. She tried to escape twice, and he threatened her with the rifle each time, but never fired it.

She thought he was asleep and made a break for the door. By the time she got it unlocked, he grabbed the rifle, she slammed the door shut, and he fired at the closed door. The bullet went through the door and struck her in the back of the head.

"Marshal, I don't deny a thing, that's just the way it happened so help me," he said when the sordid story was complete.

The man repeatedly swore by all that was good that he didn't intend to kill her.

"I can respect your belief, my friend, but you know I'm going to have to take you in. You must answer for what you have done," I told him as calmly as I could.

The man got his things together and went with me to the Commissioner's office across the river. A statement was written and sworn to by the man, just as he had told the story to me. A hearing

126

was held in Mrs. Wilson's Commissioner's court. There were no witnesses to the shooting. The evidence consisted of his statement, the gun, a bullet through the door, and a dead woman. Mrs. Wilson had to bind him over to the grand jury in Fairbanks. I took him back to the little log jail on the Kuskokwim until I could get him in to Fairbanks.

In Fairbanks, he had another hearing where he pled guilty. The sentence was light and he was released in a few months on good behavior.

Aniak didn't know the man who returned to their village. He had quit drinking, which had caused his other problems. He never caused another problem for the law as far as I know and became a strong influence for good in the Aniak community.

Bush justice isn't determined by the size of the village, nor is it geographic, but it is related to the need for and enforcement of justice in outlying sections of Alaska. For me, as Marshal on the Kuskokwim, bush justice was my beat. Sometimes in Aniak, sometimes in the tundra villages or along the Bering Sea coast, sometimes in Bethel near the little log jail, but always I felt I was sworn to uphold the law.

Clouds blow in from the Southwest in the delta country. The warm air of the Pacific attracts moisture in its northward migration and forms thick, heavy clouds. In late summer, these clouds often deposit torrential rains in sudden squall-like action as far inland as Bethel. When night comes, the clouds shut out the stars and seem to absorb any light that is left over from the day. The darkness is seemingly tangible enough to feel and a man can put his open palm on his nose and not see his fingers.

I always walked my town without using a flashlight. My eyes, adjusted to the blackness, responded briefly as I passed the yellow glow in the doorway of a prominent bar. Not many drinkers on a night like this, I thought; the rain had stopped, but the night was better for sitting at home. I headed back to my little log jail and the relative comfort of the fire.

Old Spud, my dog, sat on the steps waiting for me to let him in the house. He came to greet my familiar walk and I stopped to roughhouse him in our playful game that always ended in a stick chase for the dog to retrieve. I threw the stick and heard the dog run into the darkness. A young native boy yelled and surprised the two of us. We were so intent on playing our stick-chase game, that neither Spud nor I had been aware of the boy's presence.

The boy was breathless from running, but managed to tell me that an old lady had been raped in the house back of the Post Office.

"Marshal, she's screaming and crying and everything, you gotta hurry," the youth urged.

"I'll be right here. You go back and tell them I'm on my way." I locked Old Spud in the house, he liked a good dogfight and I didn't want him tangling with some sled team on a night like this.

When I arrived at the woman's cabin, I knew the old lady. She must have been in her seventies, and I was skeptical that anyone would rape an old woman like her. I stooped to enter the small doorway of the cabin; the scene started again as she wailed and screamed. The Eskimo woman knew the man who had raped her; he was a half-breed and had come in on her, threatening her with a knife. She had fought as best as she could, and had managed to scratch him on the face with sharp fingernails, but he persisted. There was blood on the bed where he had dripped from his wounds.

I looked out into the night; the search would be fruitless until morning. I knew the man she had named. He had no home of his own and would be staying with friends. I was sure a drunk man, sexually satisifed, would, no doubt, bed down for the night.

Early the next morning I knocked at the door of the abused woman. I wanted to look around in the daylight if she didn't mind. Outside the cabin, the mud preserved tracks leading away toward the road. Closer examination revealed a few spots of blood on the tall grass beside the tracks. The only thing in that direction was a native fish camp a few miles up river; I figured that was where he was heading.

I returned to the jail to tell the guard where I was going, then walked down the embankment to my boat tied below the jail on the river. Fifteen minutes later I tied up at the fish camp where several natives were busy cleaning fish for drying. I told them what had happened to the old woman and asked if the man she had named was in camp. They directed me to a cabin about 300 yards from the river bank. He had arrived about two hours before me and said he wanted a place to sleep.

Without knocking, I pushed open the door and entered the 12' x 12' cabin. In one corner was a stove, used for heating and cooking. In the opposite corner, on a makeshift bed, lay the sleeping man I was after, snoring loudly. I knelt on one knee and shook the sleeping drunk to awaken him. He rolled over on his back but did not awaken. The deep scratches of the old woman's fingernails were crusted with blood and the dried blood had caked along the wrinkles of the man's neck. Unable

Ethyl Peasgood displays the Marshal's cat while a young native resident of Bethel displays the Marshal's sign outside the storm entry built onto the log jail in Bethel.

Early badges cut from tin cans and fastened with safety pins soldered on the back were used to deputize men along the

Bethel stretched along the riverfront for more than a mile in the 1940s, but wasn't very interesting as a developing town even with the army across the river.

The U.N. Club at a meeting, at its annual picnic. Many of these ... (reading right to left, at its scout uniform. Many of these

Planes used the ice of the Kuskokwim River as a landing strip for Bethel in the winter. The plane in the foreground belonged to Alaska Airlines. The tarp over the cowling helped warm the engine when fire pots were used. Oil and batteries were usually taken from the planes and kept inside at night.

l'mmar often had leg race home. here three teams line up for the word to "Go!" The Moravian

Goose hunting in the Delta and along the coast attracted sportsmen and natives alike. Ted and friends display their daily bag before taking the charter Alaska back to Bethel from near Kwigillingok.

Half Springer Spaniel and half St. Bernard, Little Spudie wasn't much to look at with his long body and short legs.

Spud and the kids of the Mission get together for a Sunday picture.

Old Gand so to be looked when he patrolled the streets of Bethel with the Marshal. A highly intelligent dog, he seemed to

Headlines such as this were not uncommon as law enforcement became more prevalent in Fairbanks during the 1950's. This issue appeared on January 4, 1951, when Ted McRoberts was named acting Marshal in Fairbanks.

Marshal Ted McRoberts and his deputies in Fairbanks in the 1950's. Others identified in the picture are: Bill Bettis, left rear.

Office of the Chief Deputy U.S. Marshal Ted McRoberts as he prepares to open his desk and get to work.

Ted McRoberts, center, supervisory deputy U.S. marshal as he was honored for 20 year of service with the U.S. Department of Justice. U.S. District Judge Raymond F Plummer, left, and Mrs. Ethyl I. Lowell, administrative assistant with the Marshal's of fice assist in the presentation signed by Atty. Gen. Robert Kennedy. The ceremony oc curred January 7, 1964.

When Alaska celebrated its centennial as a part of the United States after being purchased from Russia in 1867, it was fitting that a North Country Marshal be a part of it
all. Here Ted and Ethyl wave from the back of a rail passenger car used by President
Harding on his visit to Territorial Alaska. The car is now a permanent part of the
Alaskaland exhibition in Fairbanks.

A retired Ted McRoberts finds time for salmon fishing, here he prepares three fine specimens for the freezer.

to get him to open his eyes, I reached for a pan of water on the floor and poured it on his face; he sputtered awake and sat up. I made him stand before telling him he was under arrest for the suspected rape of the Bethel woman. The man blinked with an unknowing look and offered no resistance. He fell asleep during the boat trip down river and was helped into his cell. Convicted of rape, the man spent many years in prison.

Bush justice sometimes had to deal with white-skinned violators as well as Eskimo and Indian. It was the law, not the person involved, that often created the need for a Marshal along the Kuskokwim.

Jim Cragg, my close personal friend and representative of the Fish and Wildlife department in the delta, received a tip from someone along the river that a fur buyer was illegally buying beaver skins from the natives.

The trader had a cabin up the Holitna river, a tributary of the Kuskokwim below Sleetmute, Alaska. Using a float plane, he traded with villages the entire length of the river. There was nothing illegal about buying beaver skins, but it was illegal to have someone tag illegal skins you possessed as if they belonged to them and pay them $1.00 for their tag.

The government had placed a legal limit of ten beaver to each person taking out a permit; there was open season on beaver and control was maintained by the legal limit. The trader had several trappers working for him and had collected several hundred skins. He then went into the camps and villages and talked individual natives into tagging beaver pelts for him with their tags. He paid them $1.00 for each skin tagged; ten dollars in the bush wasn't much money even then, but they still sold their tags. The trader would fly the skins out and get up to $50 for a prime pelt. When this news reached Jim Cragg, he contacted me and we decided it was time to check into these rumored activities of the Holitna river trader.

Flying to the headwaters of the Holitna, Jim and I stopped at every village we could find and questioned natives. The natives admitted that some of them had tagged beaver for the trader, and signed statements for me on the spot. When we reached Aniak we had a notebook filled with signed statements against the Holitna trader. In Aniak, Mrs. Wilson stopped being postmistress and became U.S. Commissioner long enough to issue a warrant for the man's arrest.

The trader's plane taxied to the dock for refueling at Aniak as we

145

walked from the Commissioner's office to our plane. We approached him and invited him to sit in our plane while we talked about beaver pelts—lots of beaver pelts; the blood drained from his face when we presented our credentials. At first the violator denied all allegations, but when I presented the signed affidavits by over one hundred natives, he confessed.

The law provides for confiscation of all equipment used in illegal operations involving game laws in Alaska. If the trader wanted to go out to trial, he could have taken the chance of losing everything; he opted for the commissioner's court. We filed against him personally, which would leave him his plane and equipment free from confiscation. He was charged with the purchase of illegal beaver and the sale of illegal merchandise. The Holitna trader received a heavy fine and reprimand, but was allowed to keep his business which became the most "legal" fur business along the Kuskokwim.

One hundred and twenty-five thousand people scattered throughout a territory of almost 600,000 square miles presented an impossible game enforcement problem to men charged with that responsibility. Without the help of citizens willing to report violations, most violators would have gone unnoticed. Sometimes area residents resented the intrusion of people from other areas enough to call the authorities when violations were observed.

The people of Aniak registered their complaint with Jim Cragg one day. Two Bethel men had killed a cow and calf moose near Aniak and they wanted him to investigate. Jim asked them what proof they had for such serious charges. They said they saw the men land their plane near an island in the river that had a cow and calf on it. They heard shots and now there are no moose.

When Jim contacted me about the incident, I remembered the day in question had been a day of bragging for two men who claimed they had got a bull moose up river. Their plane fit the description given by the Aniak residents.

The uproar in Aniak was so serious, the U.S. Commissioner urged me to look into the problem as quickly as possible. The next morning, Jim and I loaded our gear in the game department float plane and headed for Aniak. Jim circled the island several times and saw no sign of animal life. We docked the plane on the leeward side of the island and began what seemed a hopeless search.

Tell-tale tracks on the beach led into the woods where a moose had been dressed; a search of that area produced freshly dug ground in which we found an unborn calf. We dug up the evidence and prepared to take it back with us. Another grave produced the entrails and female organs of a cow moose.

With this evidence on board, we flew into Aniak and contacted the natives who had seen the plane and the men; they gave their statements with full identification of the airplane. Mrs. Wilson issued a warrant for the arrest of named Bethelites and we headed back to Bethel.

When we confronted the men they were insistent that the moose they had killed was a bull and demanded a jury trial in Aniak. That really wasn't wise, considering the tempers of those townspeople angry at their intrusion and killing of a cow moose, but I didn't argue with them.

Court was convened in the Commissioner's office in Aniak. I prosecuted the case with the evidence we had found. The men were found guilty; their only defense was their repeated insistance that they had shot a bull moose, not a cow. Again, the mercy of the court allowed them to keep their plane. Both men were fined heavily, and the meat was confiscated. These men learned that justice in the bush can be both punitive and merciful—a condition that made law along the Kuskokwim a fact to be respected.

CHAPTER XIII

THE CHASE

The drinking party got out of hand. One man robbed another and headed for the bush before I could be notified. He had taken the money and had stolen a river boat; everyone I questioned was sure he had headed for Akichuk.

My boat was not running, besides I needed more speed than a 10-horse outboard could give me if I expected to catch a man with an eight hour headstart.

The Catholic priest had an inboard boat that he used for mission work along the river. When I explained my problem he gladly rented the boat to me. Sleeping bag, groceries, fishing pole and rifle were loaded on board before I eased the long boat out into the current. At Akichuk, I was told the man had been there but was gone, he was heading up river they thought. Stopping at every fish camp and village along the way until I reached Aniak, one hundred and seventy river miles from Bethel, I asked if the man had been there; always the same answer, "Yes, but he's gone up river."

Having slept in the boat the night before, the Aniak roadhouse looked good to me as I docked and filled with gasoline. Everywhere I asked, the fugitive had been there, but was "gone up river."

The next morning, I started my motor while the town lay quietly in the early light of dawn. The process was repeated at each fish camp and each village that day, but the people's response remained the same.

"He passed here yesterday going up river." they replied.

However, the response soon changed to "Yes, he just left." I was then 150 miles above Aniak and five days out of Bethel.

In Napiamute, I went into the trading post to inquire about the fugitive. The local trader, Sam, was a colorful figure out of Alaska's past and a favorite friend of mine. He had come to the Kuskokwim in the early years when the Flat gold strike was made. He had been in Nome until that gold petered out, then across to Napiamute, the Kuskokwim and into Flat—later setting up a trading post in Napiamute. Sam knew everyone in the delta country. Sam's place was a good place to spend the night and find out all the news along the river. I learned the fugitive had been there only hours before I had arrived. Obviously, he was not aware that I was hot on his trail.

Sam walked to the boat with me the next morning. "If you get this guy, stop on your way back and we'll go fishing. The white fish are just thick across the river," he said.

Waving to Sam, I shoved the throttle of the inboard and headed upstream. Camp after camp the same story was repeated until I reached the last camp on the river.

"Yes, he just went into camp," they said. At last!

The surprised fugitive sat looking at me as I stood in the doorway.

"How did you get here Marshal?" he said meekly.

"The same way you did, let's go," I said.

The river chase had lasted from Bethel to Georgetown Village but I had my man. The trip back to Bethel sure looked like a long boat ride. Handcuffing the prisoner and putting him in the front of the boat, I decided Sam's fishing offer might be the one thing that would make the trip home bearable. We pulled into the dock at Napiamute and I took my prisoner to Sam's trading post. There I hired a native man to stand guard over my prisoner during the night, while I listened to tales of white fish that made me forget the hard trip ahead.

The next morning, Sam acted as navigator as we crossed the river and anchored below a native fish camp. The natives were cleaning salmon in the river above us and throwing waste in the river. Salmon eggs are natural food for white fish, which were making the water foam with their activity.

The first cast I made had barely touched the water's surface when a large hump-backed white fish weighing over eight pounds tore into the salmon eggs on my hook. Cast after cast netted white fish—the smallest just under six pounds—until I decided I had all I could take home. We hired a boy to clean the fish and I relaxed another night before taking my prisoner to jail.

The chase had taken five days to get to Napiamute going upstream. I was surprised, experienced as I was, at the speed of the return trip. The water was deep and river broad; without any stops I made it home in one day.

My reputation as the Marshal of the Kuskokwim, and the fairness of the Commissioner's court, was well-known and often proved the source of justice.

My prisoner pled guilty before the U.S. Commissioner's court. He answered every question truthfully.

When I first went to Bethel, several of the prisoners requested jury trials. Each drew the maximum sentence for the crime of which he was accused. The word got around and soon jury trials were never called for unless the case was bound over to Fairbanks. The Commissioner was fair, and I tried to be fair,too; the people trusted us for justice with little complaint. Our reputation was known in Fairbanks by the higher courts, too.

When I had to wire for special permission from the Fairbanks office, the U.S. District Attorney seldom questioned any request. If a prisoner needed clothes, I purchased them with my money and then asked for reimbursement; it always came. I wore my badge as a fair marshal and I usually got my man. The job was not easy, but it was effective. Law was respected on the Kuskokwim because we tried to be fair and honest with everyone.

CHAPTER XIV

WIFE KILLER

Radios brought warmth and joy to the lonely cabins in Alaska's arctic wilderness when the winter cold held our world in its grip of death. Radios were the ribbons that tied the outside world and reality into one neat package and sustained our sanity when cabin fever tried to crush the soul between the log walls of a 12-foot square enclosure.

Radios worked both ways and became communication links between villages. They brought reports of good hunts, word from family and friends, and kept commerce on an even keel. Radios were also used to call me when trouble was at hand.

I saw the man leave the radio shack and start toward my office. Outside, the temperature hovered at 40-below zero as he turned his face away from the slight breeze that sent the chill factor much lower; he was coming straight toward the window where I was standing. A sick feeling knotted my stomach; it could only mean someone wants the Marshal and I was well aware that the cold wasn't going to break just for justice to be done.

"Marshal, there's been some trouble in a winter camp out of Aniak," the messenger said, "they just said they needed you to come right away."

153

I put extra wool socks in my pack and pulled an extra pair on my feet before slipping into caribou-skin mukluks. My fur parka, with a wolverine ruff, made me look more like an Eskimo than a U.S. Marshal as I closed the cabin door behind me.

Only one plane would be covered and warmed by fire pots in Bethel, I thought, as I walked toward the building people laughingly called "the pilot's shack." Al would fly—if the price was right. Al was Al Johnson, the best bush pilot anywhere on the Kuskokwim. Cold nipped at my nose as I neared the little green-trimed shack. Inside, Al sat in an old wooden chair with his feet propped on a cluttered office desk.

"Al, I need to go to Aniak today—can you take me?" I said.

"At 50-below the guy needs to go to Aniak," Al mutterd out loud—not addressing anyone.

Al exhausted all his excuses why a plane should not fly at cold temperatures, while I insisted they needed a Marshal in Aniak that day. "It is my job as Marshal to go if I can, will you fly me," I insisted.

The red Cessna was parked on river ice below the shack. Draped unceremoniously over the cowling and propeler was a large tarpaulin reaching to the ice below. Two fire pots underneath the tarp kept the engine warm enough to start with some difficulty.

I put my gear in the storage compartment and climbed into the right seat while Al removed the tarp and pots. The engine started. Al climbed out to loosen one ski that had frozen back to the ice.

We taxied slowly down the runway, then turned and taxied back again to warm the engine before take-off. Air speed chills an engine fast unless properly warmed; Al was a reluctant pilot in cold weather anyway.

As we neared where the plane had been parked, Al turned to me and asked, "Are you sure you have to go today, Marshal?"

Gotta go today, Al," I said, smiling at his reluctance to fly in the cold weather.

Without another word, Al eased the throttle forward, and the little plane skimmed over the ice. Al began his turn immediately and was on heading to Aniak before the plane crossed the opposite bank of the river.

The story I got in Aniak was not good. Indians trapped the area above Aniak each winter and one of their teenage girls had walked into town the day before—more dead than alive some said—with a sordid story of family conflict.

Most of the trappers made their own homebrew and during the long winter days many of them drank heavily. The girl said her father had been drinking and beating her mother for three days. While he was sleeping the day before, she and her mother decided to run away. Their cabin was 25 miles from Aniak; they had no snowshoes and were afraid to take time to hitch the dogs to the sled. The trail was frozen hard and they made good time running and walking—except when one of them broke through the crusted snow; it was difficult to crawl back on top of the crust without breaking through again.

About three miles from the cabin the girl looked back, someone was coming toward them along the trail. She could tell it was a man on snowshoes, half running and half walking; he rapidly closed the distance between them, which was less than a mile, in this jogging fashion of snowshoeing. The girl began to run when she recognized her father; her mother couldn't keep up. Looking back she saw him strike her mother, knocking her to the snow. She stopped running and watched as her father grabbed her mother's long black hair and started toward the cabin—dragging her like a sack.

As I talked with the girl, I examined the collection of personal things the Commissioner handed me, including the clothing she had worn into town. Her undergarments were made of flour sacks and only light clothing had covered them. The mystery to me was how she had survived at all, yet she had no frostbite or obvious physical damage after a few days rest.

Word reached Aniak by "bush telephone", a system of passing messages from person to person that was remarkable for its speed and accuracy, that other people trapping in the area had found the girl's mother. She was sitting next to a spruce tree beside the trail—frozen stiff—about a mile from the trapping cabin.

My pilot from Bethel was eating lunch in the roadhouse in Aniak when I walked in.

"We got some flyin' to do when you finish," I said and ordered a cup of coffee.

"Back to Bethel, no doubt," Al said without missing a bite.

"No, we're going hunting—cabin hunting," I said.

I knew the bush country above Aniak. Most of the cabins I had seen from the air, or had visited along the river. I found it easy to follow the directions the girl had given me; soon we spotted a lone cabin in

155

a heavy stand of spruce. Flying in a wide 360-degree arc to look for a place to land, Al pointed to a tundra clearing about eight miles from the cabin. We flew low over the snow on two passes before All decided it was smooth enough to chance a landing, then he turned to me and said:

"Pray the crust will hold the weight of the plane when we touch down."

On the third pass, he eased back on the throttle and flared out about three feet above the snow, adding a little power as he let the tiny Cessna gently settle down. The crust held. I climbed out, removed my snowshoes and backpack from the luggage compartment, waved the pilot off, then watched the little plane disappear on the horizon toward Bethel.

The silent wilderness fell heavily on my ears as I strapped on my snowshoes. The spruce in the distance stood mute, laden with the late winter snow, and ice fog hung in misty strips near the woods. The winter sun was barely visible above distant hills as I started toward the cabin eight miles away.

In the protection of the thicket, I stood on the trail for a moment to survey the cabin a still 100 yards away. Smoke went straight up from the chimney a few feet, then flattened out into the trees. There were no dogs, no sled, no sign of life except the smoking chimney. Cautiously, I removed my snowshoes, wondering if he had spotted me coming and was waiting in ambush. I walked down the trail toward the silent cabin. Snow on the trail was packed hard and I could move more quickly without snowshoes if I should need to near the cabin. Outside the door I called, there was no response except the echo of my voice in the cold darkness. Easing open the door, I let it swing full wide before stepping down into the dark room. No one home. I stirred the fire and waited. The sound of the dogs barking brought me to my feet in a start as I sat dozing by the warm stove. Stepping through the doorway, I could see the dim shadow of the Indian tending his dogs in the darkness. Sitting on the sled in an upright position was the frozen body of a woman; I called to the man and identified myself as the Marshal from Bethel.

The Indian had gone after his wife's body to provide her a proper burial. The handmade coffin was on a scaffold in the trees behind the cabin; he had planned to have the funeral service alone the next day and leave her in this natural deepfreeze until spring. Graves couldn't be dug in the frozen ground before May or June.

Inside the cabin, I explained in carefully chosen words that I was arresting him for the murder of his wife, who was sitting frozen on the

156

sled outside. The man denied kiling his wife; he said she had just frozen to death. It was true, she had run outside in sub-zero weather without proper clothing because of his beatings, but she should have known better, he argued. I then explained that it was manslaughter and he would have to go into Aniak with me.

Another Indian trapper arrived while I was attempting to explain white justice to a brown man whose limited contact with whites left him without their logic. I told the friend who had stopped by to gather all the people who had seen the body on the trail and to bring them back to that cabin as witnesses. The Indian left without saying a word. I felt sure he had understood, but the stoic silence of natives always left me wondering if the message had gotten through.

Noise of dogs and voices signaled the arrival of a dozen people and half as many dog teams outside the cabin where I waited with my prisoner. They burst through the door in a holiday mood, each with a piece of bear meat to be cooked while they talked. No one seemed to grasp the gravity of the situation, including the prisoner, as they chattered like children at a fair.

The fall had been unusual for grizzly bears in the Aniak area. During the salmon run, grizzlies often invaded fish camps to steal fish. The men decided to snare some of the bears for food and rid themselves of intruders as well. They set choker snares on trails leading from the camps, so grizzlies would walk into them as they ambled toward their free meal. Grizzlies were strong enough to break the snare line, but the hard pull cinched the choke snare tightly around their necks and they suffocated a short distance from the trap. The men snared six grizzlies this way, providing everyone enough bear meat for the winter.

The only food prepared in the cabin was a big pot of grizzly bear boiling on the stove. Each person reached into the pot to eat until he was satisfied.

While living in the Alaskan bush, I had eaten black bear many times. The rich, succulent meat was delightful, so I took my share of grizzly from the pot with great anticipation and settled in a corner to eat. Grizzly was different, I discovered. The more I chewed, the bigger the bite got in my mouth. Several attempts later I decided the only successful way to eat grizzly was to take smaller bites, chew quickly and swallow before the bite got larger. After the feast of grizzly, 14 people lay on the floor of the cabin and slept until morning.

Dawn came clear and cold and the first light awakened me. I in turn awakened the others. More bear meat for breakfast, then the teams were hitched. The fire was put out in the stove to cool the cabin quicker, then the frozen lady was seated inside; the door was secured against animals.

My prisoner and I prepared his sled for travel; he could not understand that as the prisoner he had to ride in the sled and that I would drive. Finally, I convinced him and he sat in the basket of the sled in a very unrelaxed fashion. Just as everyone was ready to move out, he jumped from the sled and ran toward his cache in the trees a short distance from the cabin. Thinking he was trying to escape, I flipped the sled over on its side and ran after him. The native turned and faced me when he heard me chasing after him.

"No, Marshal, I not run from you," he said, "I get something from cache for you."

I watched as the man placed a ladder made from birch saplings against the platform of the cache and climbed the steps. Then the thought came to me, "He has a gun hidden in the cache, so I'd better go after him." The 12 men who had spent the night in the cabin with us watched this drama of suspense as I tried to decide the best course of action. Fortunately, I decided to trust him a moment longer.

The grinning native reappeared on the ledge of the cache with two huge rainbow trout under his arm and climbed to the ground beside me.

"You make face eating grizzly meat last night. This much better for white man food," he said as he handed the beautiful frozen 20-inch trout to me. Together we walked back to the overturned sled and righted it for the trip to jail.

I returned to Bethel and told the story to Jim Cragg of the Department of Fish and Game. According to Cragg, these were the first rainbow trout known to inhabit waters above Good News Bay. Apparently, a migration up the Kuskokwim had occurred without the knowledge of the department. The native man had caught the fish through the ice.

Five sleds and 14 people started for Aniak. The temperature was steady at minus 40 degrees; the frozen trail allowed the dogs to make good time. A good sled dog can pull 100 pounds, and each sled was using seven dogs. The load was light and soon the smoke of Aniak could be seen in the distance. I was glad to get back. The trip had been cold and tiring. A hot meal and warm bed at the roadhouse teased my thoughts until the lead sled stopped as if some hidden signal had been given. The other sleds pulled along-side.

"What are we stopping for?" I asked my prisoner, and now traveling companion.

"Tea time."

"Tea time? It isn't a mile and a half to town," I protested, but no one seemed to hear.

The people soon started a fire, melted snow for water, and everyone had tea—including me. The tea break consumed two hours. I wanted to get into Aniak, but I knew it was best not to hurry the natives. They are at home wherever they are on the trial; if it is time to eat—then it is best to eat, the same applies to tea. We arrived in Aniak two hours later than I would have liked, but everyone was in a jovial mood and willingly filed their statements with the U.S. Commissioner. I watched as the 12 men headed back along the trail without me and my prisoner. Truly a remarkable people, I thought, if you let them live their lives their way. I turned and walked into the roadhouse for dinner—willing to eat anything on the menu except, perhaps, grizzly steaks.

CHAPTER XV

WILD MAN OF KWETHLUK

The first frost of August painted the willows along the banks of the Kuskokwim red and gold. Crisp, cool air accented the warm sunshine on my back as the little 10-horse Johnson outboard struggled against the current of the river. The tide was running out; the current always ran faster when the ocean's tide released its pressure at the river's mouth on the Bering Sea.

The two-hour trip up river would have been relaxing had I not been preoccupied with the radio message received from the school teacher in Kwethluk. The teacher was new, that would account for the urgent request; what troubled me most was the number of mentally ill patients I had been called to arrest in Kwethluk in the past. There was just no easy way. Reason seldom worked and trust took time to build. A violent man must be restrained even if judged insane.

The teacher had done a good job finding out all possible information before calling in the Marshal's office—precious little that it was. I eased my boat alongside other boats tied on the rocky beach below Kwethluk.

A wild, native man was living in the brush near Kwethluk; all the village knew about him; for years he had caused no trouble. People would see him from time to time, but he had harmed no one. He had been suspected of stealing food from caches and homes, but most people were willing to share, either through fear or compassion. A tall man, thin and sinewy of muscle, his hair was matted and unkept. Those who encountered him said he made guttural sounds and noises. He had never been known to speak. The campfire stories always placed him in his early twenties. He had never attended school; in fact, he was known only by sight in the village. He was the source of many legends growing out of superstition surrounding the mentally ill in a primitive culture.

A report came to the Marshal's office because several cabins had been raided in recent weeks. The wild man was spotted leaving the scene on two occasions; the last cabin was missing food and a gun. The old people argued that the wild man didn't take the gun. If he had taken the gun he wouldn't know how to use it, they said. The argument was settled the day I was contacted on the radio. Someone was shooting at the village from a hill near the edge of town. No one had been injured, but no one wanted to find out who was doing the shooting, either.

"Call the Marshal in Bethel—after all it is his job," they said. The vote was unanimous.

I walked into the trading post at Kwethluk and asked several men to spread the word: all residents were to remain in the village or on the river. No one was to go into the brush country behind the village. If I met anyone there, I didn't want it to be an innocent villager. I need not have sent word, everyone was staying within the village until the wild man was caught.

Until mid-afternoon, I walked the brushy tundra country without sight or sound of the wild man. Once I found some tracks and beaten-down grass near a clump of alders. On the ground were several rounds of spent cartridges from a 30.06 rifle. This must have been where he fired at the cabins, I thought as I turned toward the village below. I was surprised at the excellent vantage point, I could see every house in the village from the hiding place. I decided the man was clever enough, in his insane way, to out-maneuver anyone on his home territory. I would return to the village and wait.

The Alaskan sun is warm in early September, but when the horizon robs the sky of its power, the evening chill is quick in coming. I slipped on a red mackinaw jacket to shield me from the cold and sat down near the door of the school teacher's house. Everyone believed the wild man would come again with the darkness.

162

Quietness settled on the village as I sat looking down the dusty strip separating the rows of cabins. The smell of wood smoke from the chimneys hung in the cool night air. I thought of the job I had when I was eleven years old and my father followed the bridge construction of the railroads in Idaho. Men attempting to organize the workers into unions were stealing materials from construction sites to slow the work. I was hired as a nightwatchman and given a 12-gauge shotgun. All night I sat in one place, too frightened to move, and waited for the slightest sound. Had anyone come near the supplies I was sure I would have shot them out of fear; fortunately, no one bothered the bridge I guarded.

Again, the waiting was the same. Except this time I could *feel* more than *hear* the movement in the hills above the town. I was careful to sit motionless; my eyes singled out every bush on the hills; nothing moved to indicate anything out of place.

"Craaack!"

The reverberating echo of a rifle blast shattered this peaceful scene. The sound came from all around me. I thought I glimpsed a light flash from the same spot in the alders where I had found the spent shells earlier that day.

I remember darting behind the cabin and into a draw that ran from the river into the hills above Kwethluk. Covering the 300 yards up the draw was easy; the next distance required a slow, cat-like pace through the brush until I was above the wild man. Slowly, I placed each step on the tundra moss, praying no twig would break and force a gunfight. In the twilight I saw a man sitting on the ground near the alders, rifle aimed at the cabins below. When I was within 20 feet of the gunman, I sprang toward the man with every ounce of strength in my legs. The gunman turned toward the sound. I hit him with a flying tackle. Both of us held on to the rifle as we rolled downhill; my knee caught the wild man in the groin; the pain forced the man to release his grip. I flung the rifle aside, still hoping there would be no gunfight. Unable to communicate with the man, I could only subdue him. Over and over we rolled, the wild man was fighting like an animal, clawing, biting, kicking and growling a deep guttural sound. His strength surprised me; this thin man had the strength of two. I found an opening as we reached the bottom of the hill. I thanked God more fervently than ever before that I'd learned to use my left fist effectively enough to win 25 professional fights. My uppercut caught the wild man firmly on the jaw. Stunned from the blow, the man lay groaning on the ground. I grabbed his arm, flipped him on his face and yanked his arm high behind his back.

The handcuffs in place, I sat on the man's buttocks for a moment, puffing to get my breath. The wild man's shirt had separated from his trousers, I could count each rib and vertebra along his back. More than ever before now, I was glad I'd handled him this way. The man hadn't eaten well, that was obvious, but he had survived for years in the Alaskan bush. Not many men can live off the land around them. This one seemed to have gotten strong because of it.

The skinny figure laying on the ground in front of me began to groan. He couldn't be as old as some said, I thought, maybe 17 or 18, but no more. His body odor was such that I decided to wait until he regained consciousness and walk him into Kwethluk. His black hair was long and matted, which accented the gaunt, hollow eyes now staring at me. His nostrils flared as he grunted and struggled to get up. I caught his shackled wrists and helped him to stand. The frightened animal-man tried to run, but I yanked hard on the handcuffs and sent the boy sprawling face downward into the tundra. Helping him to his feet again, I talked in gentle tones. The boy seemed to sense no harm would come to him and walked quietly with me into the village.

In every cabin we passed, curious faces crowded the windows to glimpse a quick look at the wild man of Kwethluk. They were surprised that he stood no taller than my 5'6½" as we walked along together. Legend had made more of him than that. He wore a tattered shirt and blue cotton pants; I thought I heard one woman telling her husband that the pants belonged to him. She was sure the wild man had stolen them, but no one wanted to claim anything as long as the source of disruption could be removed from their village.

In Bethel, I filed an insane complaint against the wild man and waited the disposition of the court. If sentenced, the man would be taken to Morningside Sanitarium in Portland, Oregon for medical treatment. I thought the incident was closed, and indeed, it would have been had the wild man of Kwethluk not become the only prisoner ever to escape from my log jail on the Kuskokwim.

The fourth day after the complaint was filed, a guard burst through the door of my quarters, too excited to talk coherently.

"Mmmmarshal, Marshal, the prisoner has escaped," he stammered.

"Escaped? What do you mean escaped? Did you leave the cell unlocked?" I said.

"No, Marshal, the iron bars were locked and the iron-clad door was locked too. He just vanished," the guard said.

"No one just vanishes," I said angrily, "you must have been asleep for him to get past you."

I found the iron-clad door locked and the cell door secure. Frustrated I turned on the guard again, "Did you lock these doors *after* the escape or before?"

"Marshal, I swear, I ain't touched the keys since I saw him gone."

Inside the jail, I examined every bar and along the wall of each connecting cell. The jail was secure. In the back cell, the last to be examined, I stood wondering how any man could just vanish—sane or insane—from a secure jail. Then, I looked up. In the celotex ceiling a two-foot hole stared back at me.

The attic of the jail connected with the storage room over the hallway next to the guard's room. Groceries and supplies were kept there. To reach them a ladder had been placed in the hall leading to an attic trapdoor. The guard had to have been asleep, I reasoned. I was sure the prisoner had figured the connection and slipped past the sleeping guard. Years in the wilderness, living like an animal, had produced these cat-like qualities that now served him so well in his escape.

No blemish on a Marshal's record could be as devastating as allowing a prisoner to escape—especially an insane one. I wasn't concerned that the wild man would hurt anyone; during the four days in jail he had become docile and child-like in accepting favors from me. But to let him escape!

Early morning meant the prisoner had escaped after the last cell check at 2 a.m. He might still be in town, or not far into the bush, I thought. The man couldn't operate a riverboat—or could he? I remembered the rifle argument. Maybe Old Spud could sniff him out?

My first deputy was better known as Old Spud. Old Spud was half Springer Spaniel and half St. Bernard. A strange looking creature with short legs and heavily muscled body. The brown and white spots, on hair that was neither short nor long, made me wonder if he was a white dog with brown spots or a brown dog with white spots. Whichever the case, Old Spud was loyal to his master and the best deputy any Marshal ever had.

I took the wild man's shirt that I had torn in the downhill scuffle, let Old Spud sniff it, and took him outside the jail. The dog seemed to sniff aimlessly all around the jail.

Trusting Old Spud to do the job wasn't difficult. Old Spud sniffed every house and building; I soon wondered if he was just along for the excitement and not after the wild man at all. Searching through Bethel wasn't an all day job. I didn't know which direction might be the best place to start, so I decided to follow Old Spud.

In a small clearing about 500 yards from the nearest house, Old Spud got extremely excited. He ran around in small circles that got larger and larger with his nose parting the leaves and grass. "You don't suppose that old hound really is on to something," I muttered to myself as I watched the methodical procedure. On the second wide circle, Old Spud headed into the alders with determination; I was now trailing the dog and mumbling, "If he's after a squirrel, I'll kill him."

After 10 minutes of trying to catch Old Spud, I stopped to listen. In the draw up ahead, Old Spud was growling and barking like he was on to something.

I could see the dog's tail wagging; he was growling and barking in a half-friendly way. When I approached the thicket, I saw the wild man of Kwethluk crouched in the alders staring at the dog, eyes wide with fright. I called Old Spud and began to talk to the wild man. He had been treated well in jail. I reminded him of this kindness. I told him of the bacon and eggs cooking on the stove and that breakfast was almost ready. I invited him to come along and eat before he set out on his trip into the bush. The man stared back without understanding, but the trust paid off. The wild man became calm and submissive to my voice. Getting up from his crouched position, he slowly inched his way toward me—keeping one eye on Old Spud who gave a protective growl as the man started toward me. Talking in low voice, I urged the man to walk back with me. Taking him by the arm, we strolled through town and back to the little log jail. Old Spud trotted along behind where a good deputy usually walks when the Marshal has a prisoner in hand.

I arranged for the prisoner to be removed immediately for medical treatment in Fairbanks. He was examined by a doctor and pronounced insane. Two days later he was flown to Portland and placed in a sanitarium—never to return to the delta country. The wild man of Kwethluk was the only man ever to escape from my log jail on the Kuskokwim—a near miss for a good record.

CHAPTER XVI

OLD SPUD

Rick Lance and his partner, John Beck, were bush pilots in Bethel who flew airplanes to earn money to mine their claims in the hills above Bethel. Like most of us who searched for the elusive "big strike", it never came for them either.

I liked Lance and Beck. They were of the free spirit that had tugged strongly at me all of my life. Rugged men of trust and character who believed in their own strength and ability to cope with the Alaskan elements and survive. I stopped at their claim every chance I got just to bring a bit of news and talk about how bad the mosquito crop was in the back country—and of course of the strike that might come today, tomorrow, or next season at the latest. I knew the frustrations of a miner and they knew the frustrations of a regular job; we understood why each did what he did in life. Each time I left, I was more sure I wanted to be a Marshal for the rest of my life—God willing.

The creeks were still running muddy, and much too deep to work, when I stopped by their camp one day in June. Beck's female St. Bernard had just given birth to six pups fathered by a Springer Spaniel owned by Lance. The argument was running hot in camp when I arrived. Beck was accusing Lance's dog of being a promiscious pup and Lance was insistent that Beck's dog had become a prostitute for a moose bone. I strongly suspect that the arrival of a U.S. Marshal saved the relationship of two miners whose quarreling had gone on in one form or another for years.

I examined each pup under the watchful eye of the St. Bernard. The last one I picked up had the brown and white markings of his St. Bernard mother, but his body was long and low like that of his Springer Spaniel father. The pup had been feeding when pulled from his mother but he immediately cuddled in my hands, whimpered a few times, and went sound asleep.

"I guess I'll just have to have this one," I said, putting the sleeping pup next to his mother.

When Beck came out of the hills after the first snow fall in September, he stopped off at the log jail and presented the little brown and white puppy to me to serve as my First Deputy.

"He's just a little 'tater' ain't he?" Beck said when he gave him to me.

"A little bit of a spud is right," I agreed. So, Spud he became from that moment on to everyone who knew the Marshal's First Deputy in Bethel.

Springer Spaniels are black and white dogs with fairly long hair, at least Spud's daddy was. He had a long body with short legs and was a good hunting dog. He loved the water and seemed to enjoy jumping in the creek, river, or nearest waterhole. This much Spud took after his father.

St. Bernards are big brown and white dogs with huge heads and powerful jaws; at least Spud's mother was. Beck swore that old dog could understand every word he said. In fact, it got to where he had to spell to outsmart the dog, but then she learned how to spell, he would brag.

Spudie had the best of both dogs. He had the natural smartness that made my training look professional. By instinct he survived and won against great odds.

I first noticed this quality before Spudie was three months old. He was playing in the yard near the jail when some wild sled dogs got after him. These malemutes are easy death to any strange dog that crosses their path. As a pack, they will fight any outsider; little Spudie saw them coming—too late to reach the house, or the jail.

I had made the prisoners dig drainage ditches during the summer to drain the property near the jail. The ground was all permafrost and chipping the ditches a foot deep had been backbreaking work. The warm summer sun did more than the prisoners, once the surface layer had been disturbed; they were now two feet deep and the tops had closed until they were only about eight inches wide.

Realizing he could not get to the house, Spudie jumped into the ditch and began to move down the ditch toward the house. I heard the dog commotion and rushed outside. There were five malemutes digging and biting at the sod overhang that protected the pup beneath. I fired my pistol into the air, and the malemutes fled like five grey streaks in five directions. I knelt beside the ditch and lifted little Spudie out. The pup seemed to sense that I had saved him from a fate worse than death. From that moment on we were inseparable friends.

Little Spudie had trouble learning not to use the house for a bathroom, but he did learn to hide when he heard me coming, if there was a puddle somewhere in the house.

The first winter Spudie became Old Spud. He grew longer and longer, but very little taller. His head became massive and his jaws could hold my leg without hurting, yet were powerful enough to prevent me from freeing myself. His ability to trail was natural. He often used this quality to find me in the pitch black nights when spring storms began bringing rain to the delta country.

One night I made my rounds to check the town before going to bed. I called Spud, but he didn't come, so I left without him. Walking the full length of town, I saw a light on in Rev. Ditmer's residence. I knocked on the door to inquire if anything was wrong since they normally went to bed early. They assured me nothing was wrong, and invited me in for a hot cup of coffee. The night chill made the offer sound too good to refuse—besides I hadn't visited with my friends for a long time. I stayed nearly an hour then started back along the boardwalk. One of the fishing boats docked nearby had a light on in the cabin; I recognized the boat and knew it had just pulled in. Going on board, I knocked at the cabin door. The two brothers were glad to see an old friend. We had known each other for a long time. They offered to share their late-night supper, but I refused. Finding everything secure, I then went back to my cabin. Spud still was not home, so I went back into the night to look for him. Loose dogs were still a nemisis to keeping the peace—even if it was the best dog in town.

The light was still on at the Ditmer's house. I knocked and asked if they had seen my dog.

"Why yes, Marshal, he came here and scratched on the door. We let him in and he went through every room and then scratched to get out, so we let him out," Reverend Ditmer said.

I figured Spud was looking for me and began to retrace my steps. At the boat the story was repeated. They had seen Spud, he scratched on the door, they let him in and fed him, then he wanted out and left.

When I got home, there sat Spud on the steps, whining to get in. He was never taught to trail, he just did it.

Spud got his education on the streets of Bethel. He learned to fight for survival as a pup. The dog law was difficult to enforce, and there were many sled dogs that roamed the streets at night. Spud's quickness of movement and powerful jaws sent many sled dogs scurrying away with torn ears, and shoulders laid bare to the bone. Spud became very protective of his master as he grew older, and more than once helped me make an arrest.

"He is my best deputy," I often told folk when asked why I didn't leash my dog on patrol.

The roadhouse owner sent for the Marshal during a disturbance one night. A big Norwegian fisherman from Bristol Bay had followed the Eskimos back to Bethel after the canneries had closed along the coast. Most of the Eskimos from the Kuskokwim went to the coast to work in the salmon industry during the summer season. When they returned with money and the whites who followed them back, trouble always came with them.

The big fellow from Norway was over six feet tall and muscled from hard work at sea. When they summoned me, Spud went along. The dog sat beside the door and waited as I went in after the big drunk. Some of the men in the bar helped me subdue the big man and get him into the street. He wanted to fight, but the numbers discouraged him until I started for the jail without help. The big man became belligerent and began to curse me with every bad word he knew in English and Norwegian.

Out of sight of the roadhouse, the Norseman decided he could take a 5'6½" Marshal apart and teach him a lesson. I saw his movement out of the corner of my eye and ducked by instinct as the big fist flew past my head, knocking my hat off. Before the swing was complete,

Old Spud's powerful jaws sunk his teeth into the man's leg. I drew my .38 special with tear gas bullets and shot the big man squarely in the chest. Spud refused to let go until I had the man subdued. The Norwegian knew when he was outnumbered and went to jail without anymore trouble. Spud never let him get more than a step ahead until the ironbarred door swung shut in the log house jail.

September is a miserable time of year in Bethel. The fall rains blow in from the Bering Sea and nights are dark and cold. I always patrolled the streets before going to bed regardless of the weather. The lid was tight on the town, and the only way to keep it tight was to be there when trouble started. On nights like this, Spud would usually serve as an early warning system for me. A flashlight was standard equipment for patrol, but it also made me an easy target. I didn't use it unless necessary.

Intoxicated people on the streets were sent home. If they did not go, they went to jail. One Marshal and one man, the odds could be handled; one Marshal and several men and trouble was wrapped in a big package. I kept my line short all the time and trouble never got on top. The late night patrols were one of the only answers—miserable as they were.

I pulled my collar tight and lowered the brim of my hat against the rain that had been falling since dark. The streets were ankle deep in mud and all drainage ditches were filled to the brim. The town was quiet except for the juke box in a local saloon. Spud and I left the lighted area and headed toward back streets along Honey Bucket Slough. When I realized Old Spud had left me, I stopped and listened, then called his name. When Spud heard his name, he began to growl in a deep gutteral growl that signaled something was wrong. I slowly walked toward the growl, past an open space and off the street into a vacant lot. I turned on my flashlight and saw Spud pulling something in the mud and growling with each tug. When I reached him, I discovered an Eskimo man in a drainage ditch almost filled with the icy water. The man was passed out. Spud had dragged his body clear of the water and would have had him out of danger in another pull had help not arrived. He seemed to know that he had to get the man out of the icy water; I packed the drunk man on my shoulders as we started for the jail. Spud would run ahead about fifteen feet, then turn to check on our progress. When we reached the jail, Spud lay in front of the cell door all night, as if to keep check on the man whose life he had saved.

Spud had one short-coming—he was a thief! He loved to carry sticks in his mouth, like most dogs, except Old Spud carried two by fours, firewood or any loose wood, home with him. Once he dragged a twelve-foot two by four from the hospital to the jail—a little over a mile in distance.

Children in the neighborhood knew where to find their balls if the game was stopped from a long fly toward Spud. He would sit on the steps of the Marshal's house and watch the children at recess. The minute a ball was overthrown, or a fly was missed, Spud was gone like a shot and never lost a race. The knock on the jail door, or the Marshal's house, and some child saying: "Marshal, Spudie got our ball," was a weekly occurrence. Once he carried the game too far.

The Fourth of July picnic consisted of most of the 600 residents in Bethel. The highlight of the day was a baseball game between the residents with teams dividing early in the week of the Fourth. Fun arguments became heated arguments that could only be settled on the afternoon of the day that Casey stood at bat on the old airstrip, a long half-mile from town.

I sat with Spud beside me, watching the highly contested game that was tied 3-3 in the second inning. Someone hit the ball much too hard and over the left fielder's head; it bounced on the hard dirt runway. Spud was off like a shot. He beat the outfielder to the ball by two yards. Around the field he ran with the outfielder after him. The other players joined the chase, soon everyone was trying to catch Old Spud. I had long since ceased to yell at him for Spud wasn't stopping for anyone. As the crowd got larger, Spud decided the odds were too great and headed for town with half the team after him. The crowd melted away and the game was never finished. Spud was the only thief in Bethel to stay out of jail—but then he was the Marshal's friend.

Things changed for Spud in 1954, just before he was ten. I had been called to Fairbanks a second time to fill the Marshal's post when the political office was vacant. Spud went with me. Flying on a plane—next to the window—was the only thing he liked better than chasing balls. He would sit for hours on end in his own seat on the mail plane when I rode the airline into Fairbanks. He particularly liked to land and take-off in the old Pilgrim airplane.

As a city Marshal, there was no time for plane rides and Spud didn't have the freedom of smalltown life in Bethel. I decided to move to a cabin I owned on Small Track's Road several miles out of town. There, Spud found some of the happiness he had left in Bethel.

Summer passed fast in the dog's life Spud led that year. While I was at work, he had the freedom of the woods and life was easy and good.

As fall came, a routine developed between me and Old Spud. He wasn't as active now, but each morning I would get up early and build a fire in the wood stove. Spud would go outside and I would go back to bed to wait for the cabin to warm.

The frost had turned the leaves golden, and ice had formed thirty feet out on the nearby Chena river. Spud went out one morning and didn't come back at breakfast time. After I finished eating, I went into the woods, calling Old Spud as I walked. This wasn't like Spud. There were lots of snares on trap lines in the area; I checked them all.

Deciding I had to go to work, I had started home along the river when I spotted Old Spud's tracks along the bank. My heart jumped as I began to walk faster and call Old Spud. At one point the bank became steep and Old Spud's tracks turned out on the ice. I looked with horror as I realized the tracks led onto the ice but none led back. Spud knew the ice, but he trusted it too far.

I was never a man given to tears, but the ache in my throat spoke grief words could not say. All day my mind went back to the scene on the river ice—maybe they weren't Spud's tracks! Maybe he would be in front of the cabin when I got home. I left work early that day and drove the distance home in hope. The front step was empty. I called Spud's name as I walked toward the door, but I knew they were empty words. Spud was gone.

173

CHAPTER XVII

CLEAN UP OR CLOSE UP

I sat staring out the window as a dog fight erupted among the team of malemutes standing in front of the Bethel jail. Their driver, who had brought the telegram to me, and stayed to visit awhile, heard the fight and rushed outside. He grabbed each dog by its harness and pulled them apart, yelling something in Yupiaq, which I did not understand. The fight over, the driver was preparing to leave, but before he could turn his sled back onto its runners the two angry dogs were chewing and growling in a furry ball again. The driver kicked the white bitch, catching her under the chin and flipping her on her back. His fist caught the other dog squarely on the nose and the fight ended again.

I caught myself smiling as I reread the telegram I held in my hand. Marshal Stanley Nichols of the Fourth Division had resigned. Should I proceed to Fairbanks immediately and assume the responsibility of Marshal until a new one could be appointed as the telegram requested?

The request was not binding. Everyone knew the Marshal's office would be filled by political appointment as soon as possible. President Truman would name a democrat; and I was a charter member of the 49er Democratic Club, but other political friendships would be considered. The telegram recounted my years of dedicated service and experience and the need for me to step into this position of leadership at this particular time — would I accept? I really did not know as I pondered the message.

Several factors caused me not to be jubilant as I looked again at the telegram. I was a small-town marshal, a country boy by preference. Fairbanks had 10,000 people in it, and the Fourth division was larger than Texas.

The December wind blew my parka ruff close to my face as I walked toward the school apartments. When I had a personal decision to make that involved great responsibility, I usually shared it with Ethyl Peasgood. Ethyl had been responsible for my acceptance of Jesus Christ in Takotna the first spring I was there. Her faith was the strength I needed now.

"Ethyl, I don't know if I'm qualified for a job like this or not," I argued."

"Listen, Ted, I've known you nearly 14 years, and you have done everything you set your mind to do. The question you must settle is not if you can do the job. You must decide if this is the way God wants your life to go," she kept reminding me.

After the supper dishes were done, I didn't mention the job again. I excused myself from the company I enjoyed very much to find privacy for my thoughts; I must let the District Court in Fairbanks know my decision in the morning.

I tossed and turned in the darkened cabin long after the light was out and the cabin began to cool. The fire banked in the wood stove usually lasted until about 2 a.m.; I thought, the night must be nearly over. I prayed again for God's leadership.

Old Spud sensed that something was wrong with me; he walked to the bed and whined softly. I thought it strange that Spud would want outside in a blizzard of wind and snow, but I threw back the covers and walked to the front door; Spud followed. When the door was opened, Spud tucked his tail and headed back into the bedroom.

"You must be as worried about things as I am," I said and reached down to scratch behind his ears. The dog lay down beside the bed and seemed to be content.

I said aloud, "God, I just don't know. I've got to know tomorrow." I then lay still for a long time as that prayer kept repeating itself over and over in my mind until I went to sleep.

The smell of bacon cooking always made Spud "talk" to me in an effort to get his share of the succulent food. When he whined, my mind suddenly recalled the telegram of the day before; I had completely forgotten about the Marshal's job in Fairbanks. Just as quickly as the thought came back to me so did the answer. I should go to Fairbanks and take the job! The feeling of release was so invigorating, I gave Spud all the bacon and hurriedly ate my oatmeal before heading for the Alaska Communication System telegraph office.

The Christmas season always brought warmth and joy to close friendships along the Kuskokwim. The Eskimos exchanged Eskimo ice cream, a mixture of tallow and berries, and white folk got together to celebrate in their custom. This Christmas was special to me; I had to report to Fairbanks on January 1, it might be awhile before I could return to the delta country. The Moravian missionary, Rev. Douglas Schattschnieder, was going to the Mission Orphanage in Kewthluk for Christmas; he invited Ethyl and me to go with him. We could spend Christmas Day with the children and missionaries and return the day after Christmas; the thought pleased me immensely.

The dogs ran well on the wind-packed snow in the middle of the Kuskokwim ice. The great white highway glistened in the brief sunlit day of winter — one of the few calm days we had experienced that month in 1950. Doug broke trail since his sled was lighter; Ethyl rode in the "basket" of my sled. We ran along behind the sleds when the going was rough and "rode the runners" when the trail was smooth. We arrived in Kwethluk shortly after lunch.

Christmas Eve was greeted by a strong southwest wind blowing up the Kuskokwim from the Bering Sea. The warmer, moist air collided with the cold stillness of the interior and huge snowflakes began to stick against the sides of the orphanage buildings. Swirling wind stuck snow under the eaves, on the bottom side of tree limbs and drifted the white stuff on the leeward side of everything. Christmas Day was little different; the storm continued. For three days we looked at the low hanging clouds and listened to the wind for some telltale sign of abatement.

I paced the floor without intending to appear nervous. I really wanted to get to Fairbanks before January 1; the new job held enough anxieties without reporting late.

The morning of December 27, 1950, was as peaceful as the pictures on the Christmas cards ringing the orphanage doorway. "Rev. Doug," as the natives sometimes called him, and I broke our sleds out of the packed snow and turned them on their sides while we cleaned frozen crust from the runners. The soltice sun struggled above tree tops and painted the white country in delicate pink. Dogs rushed against their tethers, anxious to run after three days of hibernation.

Both sleds were loaded and the last farewells were being said when Doug's team lunged forward. He didn't stop them, but yelled "hayaee" as the full strength of the dogs lunged against the stringer. He turned to wave at the smiling group in front of the orphanage, then disappeared down the riverbank out of sight.

Ethyl and I closed the distance between the sleds easily; Doug was moving more slowly breaking new trail. We followed about 100 yards behind until we were halfway to Bethel. Doug pulled his team to a stop and we stopped right behind him. The panting dogs bit at the snow to replenish the moisture in their bodies. Even though they are trained to bite snow to the side of the trail as they run, they seem to need extra snow when they stop on the trail.

"Everything going alright?" I called to Doug as our sled stopped abruptly.

"Going fine. I thought we might let Ethyl stretch her legs while the dogs get their wind," Doug said. "They are running on top most of the time, but there are soft spots in places."

Ethyl got out of the basket to stretch and get circulation moving in her legs. Five below temperature can quickly chill a person sitting still in a sled.

Doug was anxious to get home and called his dogs into motion as Ethyl was getting seated. Seeing the other dogs leave excited my team and they began to bark. I yelled and each dog tightened his harness almost in unison. I said to Ethyl, "Why can't they get together like that every time," as we glided over the new trail Doug's sled was making.

For a half-mile the dogs ran smoothly on the crust of the wind-packed snow, then I saw the back of Doug's sled sink low and water splash. Doug's sled had run into overflow! "Overflow" occurs when water levels drop beneath river ice, causing it to sag and crack midstream. Water flows up through the crack; if covered with much snow, it won't freeze. Often this condition can't be seen from on top of the snow and creates a life-threatening hazard for any unwary traveler in sub-zero weather. Doug was yelling and pushing his sled trying to avoid the frozen slush that his team had pulled him into. His boots were wet but he hadn't gone in the water deeply. I tried to turn my team, but they were on trail and followed the other sled. The first of my dogs made it through okay, but when my sled's weight hit the mushy ice trap, I sank to my thighs in icy water. Yelling every breath, I urged the dogs to extra effort for another 30 feet. They sensed the emergency and strained every muscle to keep pulling. Ethyl sat helplessly in the basket as the ice water seeped through the covers. The sled pulled up on top of the firm snow as we neared shore. Finally on the bank, the two teams stopped.

"I'm going to have to dry my feet or they will freeze," I said. "Since I got my toes frost-bitten a few years ago I can't stand much cold on them."

"It's not my feet that I'm worried about," Ethyl replied, feeling her wet clothing.

"Well, there is no wood right here; let's move on to those trees," I said, pointing to a thicket a quarter of a mile down river.

Doug had extra socks that I could wear — my dry socks had been under Ethyl in the sled. We built a fire and dried as best we could. All of us felt it was unsafe to return to the river ice; the only way for us was to break new trail along the bank. The trip was slow going through draws and thickets, but much safer than on the ice, we felt.

The mail run to Fairbanks left Bethel on Saturday morning, December 30, 1950. The pilot flew his old single-engined Pilgrim with the finesse of a master. The weather had turned bitterly cold as clear skies returned to the delta country. The plane didn't have a heater of any kind in it. Both of us wore so many clothes in our effort to defeat the chilling cold we had to sit in the seat and swing our feet into the cockpit. The mail plane stopped at every village between Bethel and McGrath that had a strip—and most of them did. All day we landed and took off into the numbing coldness of late December Alaska. I would open the door and drop the mail sack; if the villagers had any mail to go, they ran to the small plane before we could turn around and head into the wind. Usually, there was no pickup and I was grateful for not having to open the door to the wind blast of the propeller a second time.

Darkness was blending the black-colored spruce into one mass as the mail plane approached McGrath. The pilot could have landed on that strip with his eyes closed had he wanted to. Without lights on the ground, I couldn't tell where the runway was until I heard the snow and rocks kicking against the fuselage. We tied the Pilgrim to the ground, grabbed the McGrath mail sack, and walked to the Roadhouse/Post Office/General Store/Restaurant to spend the night. Stiff from the numbing cold, we walked like mechanical men into the warmth of the welcomed Roadhouse.

The pilot's contract didn't call for as many stops between McGrath and Fairbanks, but it still took most of the daylight hours to reach Weeks Field in Fairbanks. Darkness had settled on Second Avenue when I walked through the lobby doors of the Nordale Hotel and asked for a room.

The next morning was New Year's Day. For most of the law enforcement officers, New Year's Day was anything but a holiday. Fairbanks was a wide-open town for liquor, gambling and prostitution without the added attraction of New Year's Eve. I knew most of the deputies working in Fairbanks from previous trips to town; they greeted me warmly.

"Ted, Judge Pratt wants you to call him as soon as you check in, I think it's about swearing you in as Marshal, " one of the deputies said. I checked the telephone book for the number and dialed Judge Lewis K. Pratt at his home.

"Judge Pratt? This is Ted McRoberts, Deputy Marshal from Bethel. I just checked in with the Marshal's office here in town and they said you wanted me to call you even though today is a holiday," I told the Judge when he answered the phone.

"Glad you did, Ted. You know Nichols is already gone...outside someplace, and we need someone in charge here. I'll be right down and swear you in," Pratt said.

Judge Pratt read the swearing-in ceremony and charged me to uphold the laws of the Territory of Alaska as U.S. Marshal. The words were almost the same as the ceremony eight years before when I became a Deputy Marshal on the Kuskokwim. Pratt wished me good luck and returned home to finish the New Year holiday. I used the rest of the day to talk to the deputies on duty, go through the files, and become familiar with the routine of the Marshal's office of the Fourth division.

I was surprised to find that rumors were often true concerning the conditions in Fairbanks. Gambling was wide open. Many businesses had slot machines sitting between the cash register and the front door. I watched in one business place as the customers placed their change in the one-armed-bandits. The wheels spun rapidly, the bell clanged faintly as each wheel stopped its spinning, and the disappointed patron walked out with a shrug of the shoulders. Ten customers passed the machines as I watched, seven put coins of some denomination in one of the machines—some played more than one machine.

In 1951 Fairbanks, had silver dollars in circulation. Change frequently was made with silver, but few people seemed to notice the extra coinage unless they paid for a 20 cent package of cigarettes with a $20 bill and got 19 silver dollars in change. The slot machines were in every silver denomination from five cents to $1. Some places had all five sizes in a row—and frequently beside the front door, where customers were tempted by impulse to try their luck. The bars and nightclubs had rows of the machines set up for their customers too. The businesses depended on the receipts of the machines to keep their operations going.

Punch boards were in more businesses than were slot machines. Some grocers kept punch boards available for their patrons—just in case the housewife, or casual shopper, had an urge to take a chance. The boards were smaller than $1 per chance—some as small as five cents, but all paid off in money or prizes; the prizes were an effort to evade the existing laws against gambling.

After two days of observation throughout the city, I felt I knew what must be done. I had a strong belief that my sworn duty was to uphold the laws of the Territory of Alaska and of the United States. I felt the legislature had made the laws, and if the people didn't like them they could change them through the legislature. To write a law and turn your head to keep from seeing its violation was not the way I had been reared, nor the way I had learned to marshal on the Kuskokwim.

"Marshal, if you close down gambling the whole town will be against you, you know that?" one of my deputies tried to counsel me.

"Yes, but I also know that the villages outside of Fairbanks can't understand why we enforce the gambling laws on them and let it run free in town," I argued.

"But Marshal, it's more than just gambling here in Fairbanks," the deputy continued, "these merchants and businesses will be hurt without this source of revenue."

I didn't answer. I left word I could be reached at my room in the Nordale Hotel and walked into the cold air of the early evening; the coldness only agitated my feelings as I hurried down Second Avenue. A decision had to be made soon. A man must live with big decisions, I thought, but he also must live with himself too. I needed help. I wished Ethyl were in Fairbanks, I needed her counsel and assurance, but this time I couldn't turn to her strength.

I stood beside the window in my darkened second-floor room in the Nordale. The lights along Second Avenue seemed as mute sentinels reminding me of the gambling behind the closed doors of the bars and buildings along the street. The weight of the decision brought a chill to my room. As I shivered, I reasoned it could be nothing else. The temperature was 13 below as I entered the hotel. I had glanced at the Syrup of Black Draught thermometer beside the hotel entrance an hour earlier.

Sometime before midnight, I turned and walked to the edge of my bed. I knelt on both knees beside my bed and began to pray. The clock down the hall struck midnight before I stood to my feet and walked back to the window. The Lacey Street Theatre lights cast my shadow the full length of the wall on the opposite side of the room. I saw my shadow move and smiled.

"I wish I was that tall right now," I said aloud looking at the ten-foot shadow my body made.

Several times before morning, I returned to the beside where I had erected my altar, to lay my problem before the God who had cared for me since my commitment in the spring of 1937. The deep moments of prayer caused me to lose track of time, and the minutes expanded into hours. I heard the clock strike four times and stop. I lay across my bed fully clothed and slept until 6:30 a.m.

I stood to my feet, walked to the window and looked over the sleeping city. I knew what I must do at 8 o'clock that morning. The decision was crystal clear in my mind, I wondered how the agony could have been so great a few hours before.

I arrived at the office at 7:45 a.m. and called the *Fairbanks Daily News-Miner* to tell the editor of the forthcoming announcement. At 8 a.m. a reporter from the paper had already been waiting in my office five minutes for my announcement—he had run three blocks and up the stairs to the third floor office. He was beginning to breathe normally when I walked out of my office and handed him a written statement, a copy of the official order. The reporter looked at the order and ran out the door without saying a word. I thought: that poor fellow is going to be out of breath for sure and his day is barely started. I just hadn't understood what the news meant to him or his newspaper. The afternoon headlines of the *News-Miner* stretched across the eight full columns in type an inch and one-fourth tall: U.S. MARSHAL: 'END GAMBLING'. The one-fourth inch sub-head was no less sensational: *Slot Machine Edict*

Issued by McRoberts. A third lead continued the story: *All Games of Chance Banned in Division After Saturday.* A picture of me, that was to have been in Thursday's paper anyway, carried a caption continuing the news of the edict: "Ted McRoberts, appointed temporary U.S. Marshal, today issued a 48-hour 'cease operations' ultimatum to gamblers in the Fourth division." The die was cast; I couldn't turn back.

The newspaper hit the streets shortly after lunch, by 4 p.m. a delegation of "city officials" were sitting in my office explaining that the city just could not operate without the illegal revenue.

"Marshal, you just don't understand the situation. City ordinance No. 427, passed by our city council in 1948, gives the owners of slot machines, pinball machines and card tables the right to operate if they donate one percent of their gross receipts to the city every month. Why, Marshal, we get $50 per slot machine per month, $25 per 'pan' table and $75 per poker table. You'll ruin us. You must find another way," the spokesman for the group explained to me.

"I'm sorry gentlemen, the order stands," I said as quietly as I could.

Mistaking my gentle manner for weakness, another of the group spoke: "Marshal, the records show that these donations have totaled $3,035 for the past three months and averaged more than $3,000 per month prior to October for last year. We will all go broke."

"Gentlemen, I guess you will just have to go broke and start over again," I said with more firmness. "Now, if you men have finished, there is really much more work that I need to get on with." They left without anymore argument.

Notices were officially issued from my office that all businesses were to remove the slot machines by Saturday of that week or the machines would be confiscated. Most of the machines were owned by one man, and he cooperated with the order. On Saturday morning, I and four of my deputies, with the cooperation of the Fairbanks police department began checking businesses and known locations of slot machines. We didn't confiscate one machine that day. Later, after the newness of the order had passed, some businesses assumed the "clean up" would be like all others and last about 30 days. When slot machines appeared in the "back rooms", we carried them out and kept them as confiscated property. Twelve machines were taken before the businesses realized we weren't just carrying out a federal bluff.

Congress had passed an anti-slot machine law two days before I issued that closure order in Fairbanks. Senator Estes Kefauver was chairing a committee that was making national headlines inquiring into gambling. The natural assumption by many gamblers was that I was complying with the political fervor and not with the Territorial law. After they lost the twelve slot machines, the message began to get through. My deputies kept overhearing people say, "The Marshal really means business this time, doesn't he?" And I did. I had earned my brand. From the order issued two days after my first job as U.S. Marshal, I became known as the man who closed up gambling in Fairbanks. This title stayed with me for years afterwards.

When the gambling order was issued, I didn't know the pinball machines were paying off in cash. With the slot machines gone, the activity picked up around the pinball machines and they became more open with their payoffs.

I immediately assigned undercover agents to get all the information possible on the pinball machines. The file began to grow. The number of the machine, its location and specific description became the largest file on my desk. The agents would play the machines and keep close records on what they won or lost, then give me sworn affidavits. Armed with these, we got warrants and the law enforcement officers under my jurisdiction, either directly or in cooperation with the city police, swarmed over the city. Within hours all pinball machines were confiscated along with five more slot machines. Gambling was at a virtual standstill for the Fairbanks businesses after this raid.

The courts turned the money in the machines over to my office to use as payoff money in the search for other vice outlets, particularly dope traffic. The decent element in Fairbanks increasingly was beginning to worry that organized crime was entering our town with drugs and white slave traffic.

CHAPTER XVIII

BACK HOME AGAIN

I knew when they called me into Fairbanks that I was not being considered for appointment as U.S. Marshal on a permanent basis. In fact, I lived in a legislator's house and cared for it until he finished his legislative term in Juneau. But I went at my job as if I planned to be there forever, and it payed big dividends for law and order in Fairbanks. Finally, my replacement arrived. I packed my bags and prepared to return to Bethel in a couple of days, just as soon as I was sure he didn't need me any longer. On April 2nd the mail plane had room for me to ride and I bought a ticket home. I wanted to take a vacation—I hadn't had one for several years—but I thought I had better see how things were in Bethel before I left. I really wanted to go "outside" in the summer and planned my vacation for June.

I guess it was a good thing I did not leave without checking Bethel first. When I arrived, I found that much of what I had been fighting in Fairbanks had moved to Bethel.

The new owner of a local roadhouse had purchased some of the very pinball machines I had ordered out of Fairbanks. I felt the order I had issued in Fairbanks as Marshal of the Fourth division applied to all divisions, and Bethel was part of that order. I didn't bother to inform the owner of the roadhouse. I knew he was trying my authority since he knew I was coming back to Bethel. I took my deputy and hired a truck to meet us at the roadhouse. We confiscated all the pinball machines and took them to the jail and locked them in one of the cells.

The roadhouse owner immediately hired a lawyer who told me I was out of place to do such a thing. I stood firm and told him that when the courts ordered me to replace the machines they would still be in good condition. The Commissioner's court in Bethel backed me all the way. They went to the U.S. Attorney in Fairbanks. When he backed me they tried to appeal it further. I don't know how far it finally went, but I do know the roadhouse never got the pinball machines back.

I hadn't been back in Bethel but a week when I got wind that there was a prostitute in town who planned to open for business as soon as she could rent a house. I decided to find her before she got established. I met with several of the honkeytonk owners in town, and no one admitted knowing her. Then I walked into one place and the only person I didn't know was a white woman at the bar. Since she didn't know me, it was easy to get her to make her business known. I nailed her and took her over to my office. I told her there was no place for her in Bethel and my recommendation would be for her to just saddle up and move out immediately. She didn't seem convinced until I told her that if I caught her doing anything wrong around town—anything at all—I would throw the book at her. Finally, I convinced her that we had a "tough" commissioner in town and together we would give her everything the law would allow. I don't know when she left, but I never saw her around Bethel again.

Winter in the bush was lingering into April in the spring of 1951, and I had missed most of it while in Fairbanks. I had not been back in Bethel long when someone came by my office from a village up-river. He said as he came into town he spotted trouble at a cabin about seven miles up the Kuskokwim. When he arrived at the cabin he saw a man's body out in the yard and most of his dog team loose nearby. He became frightened and left—besides one of the dogs wouldn't let him close to the body.

I borrowed a dog team and went to investigate. I found things just about like the man had described. Most of the dogs stayed at a distance and barked a me, but one dog wouldn't let me near the body. I don't know if it was that dog, or some of the team, but dogs had eaten on the man's arms and one leg. I tried to chase the dog away with a large willow stick I found near the trail, but he bared his teeth and stood his ground. Finally, I drew my pistol and fired over the dog's head. He refused to move for two shots then started for me. I had to kill him before I could get the body on my sled. I have never seen a dog guard a body like that one did. I untied two dogs that hadn't gotten loose and let the team run free before I left.

The body was frozen stiff and had been dead a long time. We had no way to determine the cause of death. There was no sign of violence other than where the dogs had eaten on him.

The Moravians usually carried out burials like this for me. I tried to help in any way I could. Usually, we dug extra graves in the summer because the ground was frozen so hard in the winter. Even in the summertime, the permafrost made gravedigging a big job. Everyone used caskets made in Bethel. They were just plain wooden boxes, handmade but adequate.

We had a casket made for the man, and I got some men to serve as pallbearers. When we got ready to move the casket across the grave and lower him down, one of the fellows caved off the side and fell into the open grave. Someone quipped in irreverent fashion, "One at a time, one at a time." We stopped the funeral long enough to get the pallbearer out of the grave, then continued.

The graveyard in Bethel was a problem anyway you look at it. When first established, it was a long way from the river, but the channel of the Kuskokwim had changed and cut the bank away. Each time a storm hit Bethel, the bank of the river would cave another 10 or 15 feet.

Directly below the graveyard, a road went down to the water's edge where the waterman filled his truck with water for deliveries to the townspeople. He would heavily clorinate the water for safety. People would purchase this water in five gallon buckets for their household use.

As the river continued cutting into the bank, I received an increasing number of calls of drownings. Without exception, it was another body washed from a grave and floating in the river where the waterman got his water.

After I moved to Fairbanks years later, one of the boys I had in my scout troop, who owned his own plane, came to visit me. Ethyl Peasgood and I invited him to dinner at her place. He just kept drinking water all the time. Ethel would get up and fill his glass only to discover it empty before the meal had progressed very much. Finally, he made a pun to justify his drinking so much water when he said, "You know this

Fairbanks water isn't as satisfying as our Bethel water because it doesn't have enough *body* in it.''

Bethel was voted "dry" to hard liquor in about 1950. I had fought hard for this because one of the things that makes law enforcement difficult, in my opinion, is alcohol abuse. When I left Bethel to assume duties in Fairbanks, the first thing someone did was figure a way to get hard liquor back into town.

Arrangements had been made with Northern Consolidated Airlines to fly liquor into Bethel by the case on C.O.D. orders. I couldn't figure a way to stop them until one day the idea came to me that the sale of liquor is where the collection of money takes place. I thought about this for several days and decided to try and make it stick. I went to the Airlines and told them they had no right to bootleg liquor into my town. Their argument was as I had suspected, they weren't buying it for themselves. I told them I understood that, but they were collecting for it in Bethel and the sale was where the money was collected. I don't know if they checked with their lawyers, or just wanted to avoid an issue, but Northern Consolidated never argued after that and ceased hauling liquor into Bethel.

April and May were such busy months for me after I returned in 1951; I was really looking forward to my vacation by the time June came. My plans were to fly to Seattle and take a train down the West Coast, then to New Orleans, across the Deep South, and finally up to Washington, D.C. I decided not to give my itinerary to anyone—I might get called back for some reason. When I got to New Orleans, I changed to a bus and slowly made my way up to Washington, D.C. When I arrived in D.C., I checked into a hotel room and decided to visit the Department of Justice the next day. I was curious to see the department I worked for, I knew several of the men working there.

When I walked into the Department of Justice the next morning I felt like a celebrity. They had been trying to find me for nearly a month. My Fairbanks replacement had resigned, and they wanted me to hurry back and take over the job again.

I didn't go back to Bethel immediately. I flew directly to Fairbanks and took over the job I had left a little over three months before. This time I stayed about three months again, and on November 1, 1951, a second replacement was appointed Marshal. When I finally arrived in Bethel, I found a repeat of the same thing that had happened before, but this time I was expecting it. Immediately, I closed things down again.

Some places had heard I was coming and had voluntarily closed down their vice operations.

I don't know if it was all the shifting around, or if something was different inside of me, but Bethel didn't feel like home anymore. Many old friends were no longer in Bethel and life was changing. Ethyl had taken a school teaching job in Healy, Alaska, and I was restless. I was offered a job with the Fish and Game Department in McGrath soon after I arrived in Bethel this time. I was seriously considering taking the job when I was called back to Fairbanks. When I arrived, I went directly to the new Marshal's office to see what was so urgent as to require my coming into town "immediately".

The Marshal didn't mince his words. He said they had created a new position of Chief Criminal Deputy in charge of all criminal work in the Fourth Division, because the job was too big for one man to handle otherwise. Would I become his Chief Criminal Deputy? This offer came in January 1952 and I took it. As I went back to Bethel to conclude my personal affairs there for the last time, I wondered what the future held for me. I had been U.S. Marshal twice and now Chief Criminal Deputy all within one year. I was sure of one thing, I would be able to continue my criminal crackdown on dope, prostitution and gambling from my new office. Maybe the future in law enforcement was still right for me. I was anxious to get back to Fairbanks to find out.

CHAPTER XIX

FAIRBANKS PROSTITUTION

I was familiar with law enforcement problems in Fairbanks by now and the trauma of my first stint as marshal in a big town was avoided. I could hardly believe a year had made so much difference in a town—or in me, for that matter.

I didn't have any trouble; the local power-brokers knew my position on gambling and prostitution. I continued to keep pressure on both and pretty well cleaned it up inside the city limits. Gambling didn't seem as hard to control as prostitution. We closed down prostitution in the city, but places sprang up all around the edge of town. In July, 1951, a study was done by an outside firm concerning prostitution in Fairbanks. The report named the houses of prostitution and the bars that accomodated hustlers. An investigator went to one night spot just off South Cushman, and the madam there introduced him to one of her girls named Jane. Jane told him, "We've got about twelve girls here off and on. . . There'll be more girls here later on. . . They closed us up on Fourth Avenue a few months ago. We're supposed to be closed now, and in order not to attract too much attention, we ask all the boys when they come not to park their cars too near the place. The madam then directed him to a small improvised bar and offered whiskey at a dollar a drink.

The madam talked freely to the man from New York, not knowing he was a hired investigator. The investigator told me he couldn't keep his mind on what he was doing because every time he sipped his whiskey he thought of his boss back in New York looking over his expense account. Drinks at $1 apiece were not very common in 1951. He said these thoughts were running through his mind when he realized the madam was telling him that two other brothels were preparing to reopen. He said it struck him as funny when she kept using the phrase, "The landladies are awaiting the green light..." With the common term "Red Light District" being applied to the area he was in, it sounded more like directing traffic than prostitution.

After the investigator parted with the madam, he began frequenting the other two places to see if she was telling the truth. The joints were next door to each other. In the first, he met a madam who again offered whiskey at $1 a drink. As they talked, she said, "Any day now I'll have girls...I'll be ready here soon...I'm waiting for a couple of girls to show up—we have to get in on the payday coming up for the soldiers." When he entered into the second establishment, the operator was cleaning up the place. He casually asked when the girls would be available, and she openly said, "We have the word to go ahead now. The lady next door got the word too. She's waiting for her girls, but I have mine. See, the place has been closed up for a week - none's been here even to air it out. They closed me up across town in April. The last time I was raided here it cost me $900. Three hundred each for me, my girl, Sherry, and my bar girl. If they get me again I'll have to sit in the clink, I'm broke." Sherry came out of the back room and approached the two. "We ain't got our place straightened out just yet—how about coming back tonight? I'll show you a good time then at the usual price—$10. —There'll be more girls then, too." Sherry was a shapely girl in her early twenties. The investigator thanked her for the offer, which sounded more personal than business-like he often said.

After leaving, the investigator drove toward Ladd Field and gave one of the soldiers walking in that direction a lift. The conversation was most profitable for his investigation. The airman suggested a house on Eagle Avenue as "a good place to find a hustler." He dropped the airman at the Ladd Field gate and headed for the house on Eagle Avenue.

When he entered the "nite spot", as the G.I. had called it, two prostitutes came forward and introduced themselves as Gerry and Candy

Candy said, "I'll have a drink with you, let's go upstairs and talk things over. We can talk better up there. It's fifteen dollars for straight and twenty for french—how about an hour for sixty dollars?" He walked to the bar and ordered another "dollar whiskey" and continued talking to the two prostitutes. Business wasn't brisk at the moment, so they both came to the bar. Gerry offered him the same proposition - if he liked her looks better. While they drank, a soldier entered the door and Gerry cut out and went to him. He apparently liked what he heard and they headed upstairs immediately.

Casey, the bartender, commented about how quickly the soldier "fell for Gerry." Then he said, "There's only the two girls now. Earlier in the day there's just one, but tonight we'll have more."

The conversation continued between the investigator and Casey. Candy moved away when it became apparent the man from New York was more interested in Casey's talk and the dollar whiskey than he was in her. A big Negro soldier came through the doorway and sat beside him at the bar. He ordered a drink and began to talk to the investigator. He said, "Man, you are missing it. Some fine colored gals can be had up the street. You oughta try them."

After heading "up the street," he met four Negro prostitutes as he walked through the door. They were uninhibited in their approach. Two of the girls, Debbie and Alma, were going from patron to patron, many of whom were Negro soldiers, and propositioning each one. Alma's line was always the same, "Come on, let's date. That's what we're here for, baby. You can't go wrong for ten dollars. We don't go anywhere, we've got rooms right here."

A pimp was mixing with the customers and urging the acceptance of his "girls". He boastfully stated to the investigator, "I don't work behind the bar here, I'm the promoter. I promote business, I promote drinking and I promote girls."

This pimp was later "busted" for pimping and was found to have most of the black prostitutes along South Cushman working for him. He drove a big car and dressed in an unreal fashion, but he was a promoter—who eventually promoted himself all the way to the McNeil Island Penitentiary.

By now, the investigator was about to blow his mind. He couldn't believe prostitution was so open and flagrantly displayed. He decided he would just make some of the clubs outside the city limits without looking for prostitutes to test them as places of operation.

193

He started on South Cushman and entered one club after another. All the places were crowded with white and black servicemen as well as civilians. Unescorted Negro females were on hand in all three places and openly asked to be treated to drinks and offered themselves to him. At one such club, Betty made no bones about her purpose. "How about buying me a gin?," she said. As they drank, she came right to the point, "Are you looking for some fun? I can help you out, whatever you want—it's ten or fifteen dollars and I've got a place on 17th Avenue."

At another club, Ruth approached him with an offer to go to bed before they even had a drink. When he turned her down, she solicited a white soldier, but he wasn't ready. Finally, she accosted a Negro soldier and left with him. The white soldier came to the bar and sat down with his drink. He turned to the investigator and said, "She's a funny hustling girl. If you buy her enough drinks she'll go for nothing. She did that for me last pay day."

In yet another club, the investigator was impressed by the efforts of a Negro prostitute named Joyce. As a prospect would enter, she would approach him immediately and say, "I'll have a drink with you. How much money have you got. I only want ten from you, but I want to drink some first. I've got to get in the mood, you know. If you haven't got it, I'll be looking for somebody else." They usually had it for she was young and attractive with a personality that seemed to attract all men. One fellow said it was her "bedroom eyes" that got him.

Eskimo girls were available in each of the places he visited. Their routine was much the same—ask for drinks then make it clear they were available for bed services. Some bartenders seemed to have the same idea about the Eskimo girls that frequented their places. All of them claimed the "native girls do it for love."

As I looked over this report my first day on the job as Chief Deputy Marshal of the Criminal Division, I wondered where the key lay to breaking this element out of our town. Liquor and prostitution were closely connected, but I knew the town wasn't about to vote itself dry. One common denominator began to emerge. Practically all of the places the investigator had gone where prostitutes were encountered were recommended by servicemen. Some stated their buddies had told them about the places; others said that cab drivers took them to the "resorts". All of the servicemen we checked claimed they could get into the "spots" either in or out of uniform and, to the best of their knowledge, none of the joints were off limits.

Various soldiers repeated the same story about contacts with prostitutes. I felt I had to involve the Military Police if I was to be successful in working with the servicemen. The commander at Ladd Field had threatened to put Fairbanks "off limits" to all military personnel because of vice. He was anxious to cooperate and assured me the Military Police would be available when we needed them.

All known sources of prostitution had to be determined before we made our move to prevent them from just slipping away. Many taxicab drivers were questioned and four offered themselves as "go-betweens". Most of them just recommended brothels, but one cab driver volunteered to provide an individual "hustler".

We had heard that a big Swedish man who drove a cab could find anyone a woman. When the investigator took his cab at the airport one day, he asked him where the action was in Fairbanks. The driver wasn't the least cautious to whom he talked but openly declared his opinion. "I like that place because I get a buck for every five dollars a guy spends there."

Another driver, who solicited for another club was just as insistent that his contact had "the only spot running". Further questioning revealed that he also received a commission for furnishing trade. He said he preferred to help his own "girl" named Chickie but that she gave him a pain because she spent too much time with a guy and he couldn't find her half the time.

At one club the owner insisted, "I chased all the trash out of here, I don't need those kind of girls; I have a nice clean trade without them." He had scarcely uttered the statement when a self-styled madam sauntered into the place and became quite talkative. "I had one girl, Frieda, working for me on Third Avenue until they closed me up," she said. "I'm getting too old to start anything again. Frieda got sick on me and I've got nothing else to do but drink. Since we can't operate in town it's pretty tough, it takes dough to work outside of town."

The Club owner kept interrupting her, trying to get her to quit talking. He suspected we were there for more than a friendly visit.

With information on most of the places in town and out, I felt we had enough proof to make our move. I didn't feel the need for a grand announcement as I had in the gambling issue. Along with the gambling, I had closed down most of the prostitution inside the city limits. The laws were on the books, it was just a matter of enforcement. Since everyone was expecting me to run a tight town, I decided to start with Fourth

Avenue, the famous "Fairbanks line" that seemed to maintain a clandestine operation long after it was officially closed.

From my third floor office window in the Federal Building, I could look southwest over the city. The location of the office building between Second and Third Avenues on Cushman Street gave me an unobstructed view of the back entrances of all the houses on the Fourth Avenue line.

Summers in Alaska afford long daylight hours, consequently, the activity along the "line" began to pick up before darkness settled over the city. I was in my office late one evening and turned to look out the window for a break from the paperwork on my desk. As I sat there, I noticed several soldiers come out the back doors of the houses along Fourth Avenue. For the next hour I watched and counted the men and the houses out of which they came. A plan of action seemed to come to mind all worked out. I became so anxious to try it, I didn't sleep much that night.

The next morning I called my deputies into my office and told them what I had seen. I also told them to plan to work late that evening. About 8:30 in the evening we gathered in the office and I gave each man his assignment. I posted them at strategic points near these houses and when the soldiers went in the front doors they could not see them, but as they emerged out the back doors I would have my deputies follow them away from the houses and then arrest them. They would walk the short distance to my office where I was waiting. The soldiers were scared, being in the custody of a Federal Marshal and in defiance of an order by the General at Ladd Field. I told each man if he would sign a statement concerning his activities that evening, and name the people and places involved, I would let him go. All of them were relieved to know that was all I wanted.

By midnight, the stack of affidavits on my desk were an inch thick. I called the deputies and told them to go home, we had enough to close "The Line". The G.I.'s had been paid that day and came in record numbers to Fourth Avenue—right into our little operation. We had some of the best affidavits I had seen.

The next morning I went before the U.S. Commissioner and got warrants on all the girls the G.I.'s had named. I had their names, description, and what had happened. The Commissioner gave me the warrants with a faint smile and said, "Looks like you boys have been busy, Marshal."

"All in a night's work for everybody it looks like," I replied, holding the warrants as if they were being weighed on scales. "This may be just what we've been looking for."

Later that day, we raided Fourth Avenue and arrested ten women at one time which pretty well cleaned out "The Line's" operation. Very little happened down there after that. Fourth Avenue went out of business overnight as a place of prostitution. The old log buildings were sold at public auction. I bought two of them to move to a new location and make rentals out of them, but they were in such poor condition I immediately resold them and they were torn down. The city cooperated in this clean-up. They were supposed to have closed it down themselves but had not. The contrast between closing this vice and when I closed gambling was noticed by some. I preferred to think we were growing up as a city.

The oldest vice known to man isn't removed from any city by some Marshal's tactic, and it wasn't removed from my city either. The activity increased just outside the city limits and a few tried to operate at other locations in town. The residents of South Fairbanks objected to the intrusion of more vice and got a petition asking for more law enforcement.

About 25 persons brought a petition signed by more than 100 others into federal court to get more enforcement in their area of town. They told of screams, fist-fights, carousing, sex acts and other disturbances which they said were taking place in their yards as well as on the streets. They blamed the civilians, the military, the native girls—just about everyone—for their problems. They did name three nightclubs in the district which they said were causing most of the trouble.

I could do little more than promise to do something about the situation. I gave the newspaper an interview and tried to emphasize that we would not be able to have a "sensational" cleanup. It was outside the city and I didn't have the manpower without the city's help. We had a six-man staff, the same number of men needed to police the Fourth Division 30 years previously—when Fairbanks was a small mining town. When I counted the Territorial police, city officers, and my own men, we only had 21 men to enforce law in the enormous Fourth Division. We worked shifts to provide 24-hour protection. Our effective strength at any given time was limited. I told them if they really wanted to help, to come forward with their complaints signed and sworn, then I could take action. The District Attorney promised that his office would go all out to prosecute offenders. Together, the promises seemed to help the feelings of the group, though I'm not sure how much it stopped crime. We did our best, but not until the city incorporated the area of South Cushman and cleaned up the bars and nightclubs did we make any real progress.

One of the most effective deterents I had was an able, young District Attorney named Ted Stevens. Stevens knew his job well and backed me as U.S. Marshal when I presented cases to him. His capable performance was later recognized when the people of Alaska sent him to Washington as their Republican Senator.

I ran the Marshal's Chief Criminal Deputy job under the assumption that the most law enforcement was needed where there were the most people. Of course, citizen complaints always took preference over any other crime fighting. We cracked down the hardest on vice in the city, which meant we were driving crime into the suburbs, and started by trying to oust all of the houses of prostitution we could.

After the "No Gambling" edict I issued when I first came to Fairbanks in 1951, any crackdown I made seemed to be headline news in the *News-Miner*. I was a little surprised when I looked in the paper and saw the big headlines: "4 Nabbed in Downtown Vice Raid." The next line was about half the size of the first and read: "Marshal Conducts Raid on Downtown Log Cabin House". Then a third and smaller declaration read: "First Vice Crackdown in Many Months Results in the Arrest of Two Women; Others Frequenting Place are Nabbed".

We had been watching this little log house down by the Chena River on First Avenue in the 400 block. The traffic was pretty heavy in and out so I got the names of the girls operating there and then warrants for two of them. I then took one of the Military Police from Ladd Field and three of my deputies with me and we hit the house about nine in the evening. We caught them in the act of doing what they do in bawdy houses and arrested four people. One prostitute was charged with operating a bawdy house and her bail was set at $500. The other was charged with vagrancy and bail set at $100. The two men had their bail set at $50. In the 1950's, that much bail for prostitution scared the girls operating in town into the outlying areas.

Not long after these raids began, we arrested two women one Saturday evening. These arrests began opening the way to stop the importation of prostitutes into the Fairbanks area. With information received from the prostitutes, the Federal Bureau of Investigation later arrested two men and a woman on white slave traffic charges. They were charged with violating the Mann Act by transporting women across the border for purposes of prostitution. The Commissioner set their bail at $10,000.

The four were accused of bringing a 22-year old girl from Texas to Fairbanks for their business. Another woman was arrested with them; we charged her with "operation of a Bawdy House" and set her bail at $500. The group had driven up the Alcan Highway in three cars and were operating out of a motel in South Fairbanks. Talk began to spread that we were going to come outside the city as soon as we got all of the places in town shut down.

Those arrested often accused me of trying to get them into Sunday School because they knew I had religious convictions, but I never arrested anyone without having the law on my side and the warrants in my pocket. My personal convictions were for upholding of the law I had been sworn to defend.

Humor often accompanied the prostitution clean-up. Sometimes the humor occurred when we broke into the rooms where patrons were not expecting company, but one of the best jokes in the department came from a serious incident.

A house was operating on Third Avenue, almost under the shadow of the Federal Building where we had our offices. No one would tell us anything about what was going on, yet we knew prostitution was one of the things the house stood for in the downtown area. Some of the neighbors complained of the number of people going in and out all night long, and occasionally a complaint included excess noise, but nothing to warrant a raid on the place.

About this time, Fairbanks got a new policeman who was young and good looking. He wore a thin, dapper moustache and was a sharp dresser. I went to him immediately and talked over a plan I thought might work. Since no one in the underworld knew him yet, I suggested he go into the house on Third Avenue and try to buy services from the girls. We were sure they were there. The manager of the Northern Commercial store across the street lived upstairs in the N.C. Co. building. He frequently was awakened in the night by the Madam throwing somebody out. She was tough, and big enough to handle most men. She would call them every vile name in the English language in the process of ejecting them from her place of business, too.

Well, I arranged with this new policeman to knock on the door and arrange for services like one of the G.I. patrons. He really protested. He said he had a wife who wouldn't understand and wanted to know how long we would wait before we came in. I told him I had two deputies with me and the warrants already drawn up. We would wait 15 minutes, that ought to give him time to make his deal, then we would come in. He agreed to do it.

That night we went up to the house about midnight. He knocked on the door and she let him in without any question. We sat quietly for 14 minutes and then walked toward the door. I knocked. When she came to the door I said, "I have a warrant for your arrest" and brought my two deputies into the room. They headed upstairs in a run, and we got there just in time.

Our man had made the deal quicker than we anticipated and he was sweating. The prostitute couldn't understand why he kept bargaining with her. They would agree on one price and he would stall. She would take off part of her clothes and he would start bargaining again. She must have thought he was good looking enough for she would agree to the new price and start for the bed, pulling off more clothes. But he would start bargaining again. He said he didn't know so much could happen in such short time in a bawdy house. We agreed to cut the lead time down for him on the next raid, but he assured us that that was the only time he would be a decoy in a bawdy house. We made the arrest stick on the information we had, and the house on Third Avenue ceased to exist after this raid.

Back when I served my second stint as acting U.S. Marshal in Fairbanks I had someone knock on my office door one day. The Madam from a local house was standing there when I opened the door. She gave me a long story about how she was operating a good orderly place. She asked me to lay off and let her continue to operate. She gave me a long, sad story about how it kept the men happy and the undesirable element out of town. I told her she had to close up along with the rest, but she didn't. When I began the vice cleanup as Chief Criminal Deputy her place was booming.

We got information from different individuals, and many of them were willing to give us affidavits about what was happening over there in her operation. Some of the fellows told us she was giving out ducats to people as they came through the door, and they had to wait their turn just as they did in the barber shop. The bar was downstairs and the men would line up at the bar, get their ticket, and stand there and drink until their turn came. She sold beer and whiskey on the ground floor and girls on the top floor.

After we got these affidavits we swore out warrants and arranged for a raid on the place. We took all the deputies we had for we were not sure what we might face. The place was really busy, we could barely push through the smoke-filled room. Our warrants named the Madam and two of her girls; we ran everybody else off without arresting them. We closed the place down and locked it up that night. The Madam received a stiff fine and the girls a lesser fine each, but they disappeared after that and we never had anymore trouble out of them.

Gradually, we routed most of the prostitution from Fairbanks, even in the South Cushman area. I was never so naive to believe we "cleaned up the prostitution" as people sometimes said we did. The oldest vice in the world will find a place to operate, but we did remove the vast open trade that flourished for years in Fairbanks.

Another problem was becoming a headache for us through organized crime in the lower-48 states. Narcotics had always been associated with prostitution, but now we found it on the increase as prostitution was decreasing. Our next major cleanup would have to be aimed at the heroin traffic.

CHAPTER XX

NARCOTICS

I really believed things would become easier for me as Chief Criminal Deputy when the prostitution was closed down. I guess in many ways it did for I am still convinced that we could not have slowed the narcotics traffic as quickly as we did if prostitution had remained wide open.

We knew there was narcotic trade flourishing through the bawdy houses, using the girls as outlets, but we were never able to get the proof. It's pretty hard to do when all the action takes place behind closed doors in a place as private as a prostitute's room.

With the clean-up in town about complete, and places going out of business each week outside the city limits, I began to get more information on narcotics than I thought possible for a town as small as ours.

One day the Seattle Narcotics Bureau called to let me know two men, known narcotic dealers in Seattle, were driving to Alaska with heroin cached somewhere in their car. The undercover man in Seattle knew the shipment was for sure, but he didn't know how they were going to hide it in their car.

We contacted U.S. Customs at Tok, Alaska, and described the car to them. We told them not to search in any special way, but to inform my office as soon as the car and men fitting the description came through Tok. In the early 1950's the Alaska Highway wasn't so heavily traveled that a Seattle car was hard to spot—especially with the detailed description Seattle had given us of the men inside.

About a week after Seattle called me, Tok Customs Office called to say a car and two men fitting the description had just passed through Tok. We figured it would be about four hours before they reached Fairbanks. I sent two men out to Eielson Air Force Base and told them to radio us when the car passed. By going past the base a few miles, the traffic on the Richardson Highway dwindled to only a few cars each hour. We intercepted the car outside of town and followed them to a motel and made the arrest. We impounded their car and I put two men on detail to search it for narcotics. Two hours later they came into my office and said, "Marshal, we didn't find a thing." I told them to go look again. Two hours later they were back with the same story and I sent them back to the car for a third time. For eight hours we searched the car, the last two hours we used different men, hoping a fresh outlook would turn up something.

I was going to have to turn the men loose. We had picked them up on some small violation, not mentioning narcotics, and I couldn't hold them much longer. I called my deputies in and told them that the narcotics absolutely had to be on that car somewhere. They said they had looked in the tubes of the tires, checked for suspended containers let down into the gas tank by a wire, and had practically ruined the upholstery of the car—there was nothing. I paused a minute, trying to think what to do, then told all of them to go back and try one more time. I believed Seattle was right, and we had tipped our hand with the men by now anyway. Five dejected deputies headed back to a car they felt they knew by heart.

Sometime during the next two hours, one of the deputies was on his back underneath the car going over every inch of the undercarriage. As he approached the right front wheel, scraping the caked Alcan mud from each protrusion of metal, he spotted a large hunk of mud on the front fender. Half-heartedly he jabbed it with the tool he was using and instead of being showered with mud—as he had been for an hour—the object didn't move. He hit it harder and realized there was metal under the mud. When he scraped the mud away he found a metal container welded to the fender. Sure that they had found what they were looking for, the deputies got a cutting torch from the garage and carefully cut the spot welds on the container. When they took it to the work bench, the one with the torch said he couldn't get to the box for each deputy excitedly handling the container. Finally, he did get the lid cut from the container and inside was the heroin. With this evidence we got a conviction of the two men and the thousands of dollars worth of heroin was enough to send them outside to prison for a long time.

The Seattle Bureau of Narcotics did a great job in the 1950's by letting us know when people were coming north with drugs. We got nearly everyone of them and our reputation began to grow among the drug dealers outside. Importation dropped off sharply at first, then we began to have more difficulty as they became cautious in transporting the stuff. We had to find our own sources if we were to be successful in our efforts to keep heroin out of Fairbanks.

We got a big break one night when we arrested a Texas girl who was high on heroin in a house downtown.

She was really in a mess when my deputies brought her in. She was spaced out on heroin and hadn't eaten well for a long time, apparently.

We treated drug addicts differently when I was in law enforcement than they are treated now. We could hold them for being addicts and usually did. We didn't give them any synthetics to ease withdrawals, they had to face their monsters in their cell as we took them through "cold turkey". Sometimes we would take them to the federal hospital in Kentucky, but they tried to treat them with Methedone. This drug would give them the same "high" and when they got out of the federal detention they went right back to drugs. Our "cure" rate was a lot higher here in Fairbanks. When an addict went through "sweating it out" in a cell, they would have memories that helped them stay away from the stuff once out of jail. Sometimes they would scream and climb the walls until we would have to get a doctor to give them a little morphine to quiet them down. This was all the help they ever got in the Fairbanks jail and many of them told me they sure didn't want to go through that again.

We put this young girl from Texas in a cell and let her sleep off the "high" she was on when we arrested her. When she began to have withdrawals she came apart emotionally. She screamed and cried and begged for two or three days, then she was alright. In a few days she was through the worst of it and began to eat the food we gave her. After a week or so she was over the dope and I talked to her. She was gifted in a lot of ways, and I helped her get a regular job. She was so grateful she became an informant.

One day she gave me a call. I could tell she was excited as she told about an agent who had contacted her. She had gone along with him and set up a delivery of narcotics at her house. I asked her to come to the office, which she reluctantly did. She told me his name, what time she expected the man, and how the delivery was to be made. We were as excited as she was for the man was a big dealer in Fairbanks. We had been trying to get him for a long time. He had the elusive ability to be somewhere else or uninvolved each time we made a bust. He had agreed to make this delivery himself.

On the night of the delivery, one of my deputies, and myself went to this girl's house about eight o'clock. The weather was cold and we dressed as warmly as we could. Her house was a shack of several rooms, but only one room was her living quarters, which she heated; the others were used but one window was broken out. Behind the house was an outhouse that tilted to one side. Beside the house was an old car that had been sitting there for several years. Snow was deep and the twilight of the winter darkness cast a dim light over the yard. We had to hide if we were going to take the agent when he made his delivery. I got in the old car and my deputy went into the outhouse. We had to wait until nearly midnight before there was any sign of life around the house. When my legs and feet got too cold, I would rub them and wiggle my toes to keep circulation. Several times I raised up to tell my deputy that we should forget it, but something caused me to wait a little longer.

The car light caught me by surprise; I managed to duck down before anyone saw me as the car stopped in front of the house. A man got out and walked by where I was in the old car and to the backdoor of the house. From there, my deputy could see him; I watched the toilet door for my deputy to make his move. When the toilet door came open I jumped out of the car and ran to the open window. My deputy followed the man inside the house. He sprang from the doorway toward the man, trying to keep him from dumping any stuff he might have on him. When the deputy caught him, the man had the heroin in his hand and threw it out the window just as I got there. I instinctively caught the moving object coming toward me; it was a package of heroin. I climbed through the window as my deputy backed the man against the wall. We searched and arrested him.

When we booked this man later, I really felt sorry for him. He was an ex-G.I. with a fine war record. He had many medals for bravery. Dejectedly, he said the money was big and he thought he would just pass a few hits and quit, but each time he thought another would make him just a little more money. He got a long sentence out of that arrest, but he cooperated with us in every way. He told us where another cache of heroin was hidden in a house basement. He said some new people had bought the house and didn't know the stuff was there.

My deputy and I decided to go down there the next night and look for the stuff without telling the people. The directions he had given were explicit so we slipped in through a little back door without telling anyone. The shed underneath the house could be entered without going into the main part of the house. We could see the people upstairs; we remained as quiet as we could. The shed had been an old garage at one time. We went to the spot the man had told us about and dug into the wall by carefully removing dirt. We found 45 packets of heroin; each one contained a "hit" the dealer had planned to sell. A hit usually sold for about $25, some dealers would undercut and sell for fifteen or twenty dollars until they got their regular customers, then it was $25.

The only drug traffic we had in the 1950-60 period was heroin. In the last years before my retirement in 1969, we found some marijuana, but not very much. It was just becoming popular in Alaska in the decade of the Sixties.

One day, one of our informants contacted us about a delivery that was to be made in one of the honky tonks on South Cushman. I knew some of those places were being used for drugs, but we never found evidence in any visits or arrests. This tip could mean more than just slowing up the dope traffic, I thought, so we were extra careful in our approach.

I sent undercover men into the streets to find out all they could. We had a slush fund of money that had been confiscated along with the pinball machines. This money was used to buy information when we needed it. The fund had become large over the years as people continued to violate the gambling laws. The court had turned the money over to my office to be used in this way.

Pay off money isn't the best way to get information, but it certainly loosens tongues that would not talk without it. We used it when we felt it was necessary. We felt stopping the drug traffic was a worthy expenditure of funds. The undercover agents bought their information. When they came into my office they knew the right night, the place, the man and the delivery. The money was well spent.

South Cushman was almost solid bars all the way to 30th Street on both sides of the street. Any night we went out there the places were crowded with people. Sometimes we would go down there, especially on weekends and holidays, and the bars would be so crowded with people we would have to push our way through.

The information the agents had purchased on the streets said the delivery was to be made in a particular bar. When we arrived, we realized the bar was run by blacks. Whites went into the bar, but it had been less segregated before we got rid of most of the prostitutes in the area. As lawmen, we frequently went into all the bars and honky tonks in town. No one appeared concerned when we walked into this place "just to look around." The owner had no knowledge of the intended "drop", I feel sure.

My Deputy and I just hung around the bar, talking to whomever we could strike a conversation with, while waiting for the man the undercover agents had said would make the drop. We knew his name and had a good description of him. He was a known peddler in town, but I didn't know him personally.

Near the door of the bar one of the beer company signs cast a brighter light than was available in the rest of the bar. Our eyes had become accustomed to the dim light, but anyone entering from the street usually slowed down and allowed their eyes to adjust to the inside lighting. My deputy and I stayed well apart to enable us to assist each other and not be caught together.

About midnight my deputy recognized the man coming in the door as our suspect. He challenged the man who must have been carrying the heroin in his hand; a package went sliding across the floor. My deputy left the suspect and headed for the package. Patrons were kicking it trying to hide it from him. I grabbed the suspect while the deputy was getting his hands stomped by people in the bar. Finally, he stood up with the heroin in his hand, puffed several times, shook the package at the people who had tried to keep him from recovering it, but said nothing.

In all the cleanup against dope, we never had any trouble with military men from Ladd Field or Eielson Air Force Base. Military Police and the Base Commander had the authority to make things tough for the G.I.'s, and this was enough to keep the men in check. Dope just carried too many problems for most G.I.'s to mess with it.

One deal occurred on Fourth Avenue just before we closed the line. A tip came in that a shipment was to be flown in on board a major airlines flight.

The informant was a good man who wanted to see this type of thing stopped, if possible. We knew there had been some narcotics coming in by air packages, but we couldn't get a good lead on them. One day, I gave the informant names I thought might be getting narcotics by air packages, and I told him that if a package came for any of them to let me know, personally. The day he called my office and asked for me personally, I knew something was about to happen. He said a package had arrived for one of the prostitutes on Fourth Avenue and it could be the one we were looking for. Normally, the airline delivery boy would have delivered the package, but the informant held this one back.

I took a deputy with me and went to the airlines office. The informant led us into the back of the building and handed the package to me. We decided to open it.

We didn't have to worry about a court order in those days if we suspected dope, so I very carefully untied the package. We wanted to be able to tie it back so no one would recognize it had been opened. We found heroin in it just as we had suspected. We very carefully put the package back together; it had been easy to open, so it presented no real challenge to reconstruct it.

The girl must have known which plane the package was due to arrive on for she called to ask if a certain package had arrived for her that day. We had hardly gotten the wrappings back on when the informant told us of her call.

She said she would send a taxi down to pick up the package, and identified the taxi she would use. Our job was becoming simplier all the time in this case, it seemed. We just waited for the taxi to arrive. When he picked the package up, we crawled into his cab as if we were paying a fare. We identified ourselves and told him just what was what. He had dope in the package and we had him unless he wanted to cooperate; he had no choice, really. I said to him that we would forget he was involved if he did just exactly as I instructed. I told him to drive up in front as he would normally do. We would be down low in the back seat. We picked up another deputy and the four of us stopped in front of the prostitute's house. He was to get out casually, go to the door and knock. When she came out, he would give her the package so she would be the one having possession before we made our move. I then told him to step into the doorway and keep the door open without tipping her off. He agreed to do this.

We stopped in front of one of the little, rundown houses that characterized Fourth Avenue when the line was operating there.

Everything went as planned. When the prostitute opened the door, the taxi driver stepped into the doorway. The prostitute's normal reaction to a man at the door must have been to let him in, for she stepped back enough for him to set foot inside. Planted squarely in the doorway, he handed her the package and pretended to wait for a tip. As he handed her the package, we jumped out of the car. She saw us running toward the house and tried to slam the door shut. The taxi driver stood his ground; he didn't want any part of being charged with possession. We ran right past him and pushed our way into the room. One deputy grabbed her with the package in her hand. We took the package and opened it right in front of her and showed the contents to her. All the time she was denying knowledge of the contents. We searched the house and found other narcotics there. One deputy found syringes and all the paraphenalia that goes with a place dispensing narcotics. We arrested her and had no trouble getting a conviction.

CHAPTER XXI

THINGS BEGIN TO CHANGE

Nothing is really stable, I guess. But in the law enforcement business changes come suddenly, and their consequences are really bigger than the events themselves. I found this true in Fairbanks. With gambling virtually eliminated, and prostitution under control, the routines of law enforcement begin to characterize our daily existance.

We always had something interesting happening, it seems, but not always as exciting as going after something really big.

During my enforcement years, I was frequently blessed with good Commissioners, District Attorneys and Judges. One such man was United States Attorney Ted Stevens, who later became United States Senator Ted Stevens.

Stevens did an outstanding job in Fairbanks during the years he was there. His understanding of my job, and his sense of fair play with those we prosecuted, gained my respect as well as that of the whole town.

Stevens had a sense of humor that enabled him to relate to enforcement. One day, I recall, he was standing in his office in the Federal Building looking out the window at traffic in the street below. He casually said to another person in the office, "There goes a car that looks just like mine, but my wife has the car and she's not downtown."

He had scarcely finished his statement when the telephone rang. His wife asked him when he had picked up her car? It doesn't take a lot of conversation in those circumstances to realize something is amiss.

Ted called me and said, "I just saw a stolen car going down the street."

I kidded him a little and asked, "Since when can a U.S. Attorney look out of the window and tell if a car is stolen?"

"Ever since he has talked with his wife and they both think the other has the car," he said.

I hung up the phone and put the description on the radio. About an hour later, two men were apprehended in South Fairbanks driving the stolen car. I was glad we could be so efficient with the U.S. Attorney's car. When I called him to tell him we had his car, I asked him to please be a little more careful with his things next time—we had our hands full with the bad guys, much less the good guys too.

During this time we expanded the Fairbanks office and I moved down to the second floor of the Federal Building. We had one big room down there as the deputies room, and at one end I had a private office. Through another door you could gain entrance to an inner room back of my office; this became our interrogation room. The office of Chief Criminal Deputy had proven itself worth keeping.

Shortly after we made this move, we got word from an informant that three men were coming from Chicago with payroll checks. They had written them out and drawn them up on a "Check-riter". Their identification was falsified and very complete the informant said. They were coming to Fairbanks and Anchorage; but either Anchorage wasn't tipped off, or they didn't believe the information. Because they got in and out of Anchorage before they were detected.

The informant told us what plane they were expected to arrive on, and that someone at the airport would identify them for us when they got off the plane. We were to take it from there.

We had just formed an organization within our department called the Crime Squad. It was organized through the U.S. Marshal's office, but was headed up in my office. My brother, Mike McRoberts, was in charge of the Squad and was a deputy U.S. Marshal. The Squad had two men from the Territorial Police, and Mike assigned these two men to the case with himself.

I told Mike to spot the men at the plane, to stay with them until they started passing checks, but keep their distance. They were not to make any arrests until each had passed three checks, but to not let them pass anymore than that without interferring. The FBI descriptions were so accurate that my Crime Squad men easily identified the men from Chicago. They were met by a Fairbanks contact who took them to a Country Club out on Farmer's Loop Road.

One of the reasons men were picked for the Crime Squad was their ability to do detective work. Part of that job involved being able to tail suspects without being noticed. Mike and his assistants were as good at this job as any three men on any police force anywhere. For four days they put these men to bed at night and awakened them in the morning, almost literally. They didn't miss, and the men never knew they were being watched. During those four days, the Chicago gangsters were going about town getting acquainted. Being seen in the small town of Fairbanks wasn't too difficult in those days. They would take precautions against being followed by always leaving a business from a different door than they entered. Many buildings in Fairbanks were built so customers could walk through from one street to another. Often it was a shortcut to the next street in cold weather. Their favorite trip was to go into the Co-op Drug on Second Avenue, browse for awhile, meet people, then browse toward the door on Third Avenue. When they thought they were unnoticed, they would duck out the Third Avenue entrance and into another business as quickly as possible.

My men had to keep them in sight during this time or else they would lose them entirely. We didn't know when they would start passing checks, but our sources had been good; we were sure they would start soon. Mike would report in to me at night with the same message each time, it seemed: "We went into every business in town again today, and my feet are killing me, but they haven't made an illegal move. They are so careful they won't even "jay-walk" and everybody jay-walks in Fairbanks," Mike would say.

I don't know why none of us thought about the possible timing they would use, but we didn't. The men had arrived on Monday afternoon, one week before Labor Day. On Saturday morning, four days after their arrival, they began passing checks. Most businesses would close by noon, and the banks would be closed for the long Labor Day weekend. Deposits wouldn't even be handled by the bank until Tuesday; they were counting on these extra days to get away.

Soon after the businesses began to open for the Saturday morning "rush", if Fairbanks had a rush business in those days, these men separated and started passing checks.

Their plan was to go into a business, casually shop for awhile and make a purchase. Then, they would produce the phony payroll checks and fake I.D.s, which looked authentic to the merchants. Fairbanks' merchants weren't suspicious in the 50's, they didn't see many bad checks and never an operation of this kind. Their inexperience could have been as expensive for them as it was for the Anchorage merchants. The same gang hit Anchorage and really cleaned them out. They cashed about $50,000 there, and Anchorage wasn't that much bigger than Fairbanks in the 1950's.

Mike later told me of his frustration while watching the man he was following cash a check, each between $800 and $1,000, and not being able to make a move. My orders had been to let them cash three checks, and Mike knew we needed the evidence.

After the man cashed his second check, Mike remembered I had given orders not to make the arrest alone. These men were known to be armed and dangerous; without a backup we might get one of the deputies killed or lose the man we were after. Without today's police radios, Mike and his deputies were on their own. They couldn't reach me or each other.

While these thoughts were churning in Mike's head, his suspect entered a men's store. Mike followed him into the store. The man didn't waste much time in selecting something large enough that the merchant wouldn't want to miss the sale, and bigger than most pocket cash. Again, the identification was in order and the payroll check looked authentic, the merchant accepted the check. As soon as he handed the man his money, Mike made his move. He had noticed the man was right handed so he approached him from behind and to the right. This way the man couldn't swing across with his right fist, or draw as easily if he decided to use a gun. When Mike said, "I'm a U.S. Marshal, you're under arrest," the bad man from Chicago froze. Mike handcuffed him and walked him across the street to the U.S. Attorney's office. Within an hour the other men were in custody. All three law officers had arrested their man without a back-up. Fortunately, they knew their job well and no one got hurt.

Ted Stevens again proved that his efficient manner in office was a deterrent to organized crime in Fairbanks. We filed charges against the men, Ted got a conviction, and we sent them to the penitentiary. The merchants recovered their money, and we had met our first organized crime intrusion in a manner that held it in "check" for awhile.

As part of my responsibility in surpressing criminal activity in the Fairbanks area, I had recommended that we form this Crime Squad. The Squad would have representatives from all the law enforcement agencies in the area, including the military; this way we could move unhampered into any area much more efficiently. Besides it would bring cooperation from all agencies since they were represented, I thought.

My idea wasn't really new. About a year and one-half before, we had a group called "the Felony Squad" which had been most effective. They had broke 19 out of 23 cases in quick and efficient fashion.

The heads of the agencies had been meeting with the District Attorney occasionally to compare notes on cases, but I felt we needed the close cooperation of a Squad to do the job correctly. In August of 1954, the Crime Squad came into existence. My brother, Melville "Mike" McRoberts, who became a deputy marshal in 1951, was put in charge of the group. The Chicago check writing gang was the first big assignment of the Squad, and they handled it with finesse and courage.

Mike was a superb officer. His dedication to the profession later led him to join the Alaska State Troopers shortly after Statehood. He served with them for 11 years before his retirement in 1971.

A lot of the work as a marshal in Fairbanks became routine as law enforcement responsibilities changed. And this routineness almost caused me to lose a prisoner. I have thought how ironic it is that the only two prisoners to nearly escape from my custody were both mental patients. The wild man from Kwethluk had been the only really close call for me until I picked up a G.I. from Ladd Field.

The military called me one day and asked if I could care for one of their prisoners that obviously was in need of psychiatric help. This was not really an unusual request since we were federal employees. I kept him in jail at the Federal Building for a few days before getting permission to transport him to a federal hospital in Seattle. During this period of time, before permission to transport was granted, I became friends with the prisoner. I felt the only way to handle mental patients was to gain their confidence. If I could get to be this man's friend, he would trust me and be easier to handle. This prisoner was sure someone was trying to shang-hi him to somewhere; he did not know where and he didn't trust anyone. Finally, I gained his confidence and he really attached himself to me. He wanted to be right beside me whenever I was in the room with him.

I would never treat a mental patient rough nor would I allow any

215

of my men to treat them roughly. They couldn't help the condition they were in as could other prisoners we handled. We never handcuffed them unless they became violent. Handcuffs seemed to always agitate mental patients and destroy the feeling of "protection" we were trying to instill.

I called the deputy marshal in Seattle, who agreed to meet our plane, then made reservations for the next morning on Pan American Airways. The days before commercial jets put us about eight hours flying time from Seattle even after they started the non-stop flights. Darkness had come to a cold, damp Seattle by the time we arrived.

The prisoner and I got in the back seat while the Marshal from Seattle drove. The big city lights flashed by as we sped along the streets. I noticed the man I was guarding had become extremely nervous in these unfamiliar surroundings. A stranger driving the car, and me busy talking to this stranger instead of him, increased the pressure on the prisoner. For several days now my charge had had no problem. He was sitting very close to me as we drove along, but that was not unusual. He kept telling me someone was going to capture him, or kidnap him, or something, but I casually assured him I wouldn't let that happen.

We got onto the freeway that led around the Sound on the way to the hospital. Traffic wasn't heavy, but no Seattle freeway is ever free of cars. The thought crossed my mind once that I should handcuff the prisoner in his nervous state, I could tell he was becoming more agitated as we drove along, but I really didn't want to do that.

Suddenly, he pulled the door handle and jumped out! We must have been doing more than 30 miles per hour when he jumped. My first reaction was to go after him, so I jumped out the other side. I thought I would never stop rolling . I remember it seemed pitch dark as I rolled and I wondered where the lights were; then I thought about another car hitting me, but none did. When I finally stopped tumbling and jumped to my feet, I saw him running back down the freeway against the traffic, in the direction we had come. I could hear him screaming and hollering "Help, help!" to every passing motorist. I took off after him.

Having jumped from the left side of the speeding car, I rolled to that side of the freeway and had to cross the line of on-coming traffic. I dodged cars and jumped aside, nearly getting hit several times. The traffic never slowed. The night was bitter cold for Seattle, and I still had on my heavy top coat and overshoes I had worn from Alaska. The man I was chasing was over six feet tall and only had on a light jacket. The

216

only thing that slowed him at all was his attempt to yell and stop the traffic. For 200 yards I chased him as he screamed for someone to stop and save him. I expected someone to try and run me down, but they didn't. Not one car even appeared to notice what was happening beside the roadway. Had anyone stopped, I was so out of breath I couldn't have explained anything. My chest was hurting from running so hard with heavy clothing on, but I was gaining on him and kept going. He slowed to yell at another car and I grabbed him from behind. I caught his collar in my right hand, jerked him over backwards in the highway, and went down on top of him. As we fell I reached for my handcuffs, rolled over, and slapped the cuffs on him before he could struggle much. I just sat on top of him and puffed; I couldn't have run another five feet, I'm sure. He was still screaming and hollering as I sat there looking at him. We must have been an odd sight, but no car stopped during all of this.

I got up and kept talking to him in a calm voice as I began to get my breath. He soon calmed down and stopped yelling and screaming. The Seattle deputy had stopped the car and was running back toward us when we got up. I told him everything was alright and motioned for him to go back to the car. I felt I had a better chance of calming the prisoner alone. By the time we reached the car, he was ready to get back in with me. I left the cuffs on him; another footrace that night and he surely would have won.

I almost lost him with my big coat and boots on, but the coat probably saved me from getting skinned up pretty badly when I jumped out. I had a few skinned places and some bruise marks, but nothing more. Strangely enough, the prisoner wasn't skinned much worse than I was. How we managed to leave a car doing 30 miles per hour on a concrete freeway and not get beaten up in the process will remain a mystery.

We walked into the reception room of the American Lakes Hospital and I felt the reaction. When we saw ourselves in the light, I felt the need to do a little explaining. The attendant seemed to think that coming from Alaska, looking as we did was perfectly in order. I'm really not sure he ever believed my story after I finished telling it.

"Do you realize you dived out of this car at better than 30 miles per hour in the midst of traffic," my deputy friend was saying. "Why didn't you wait for me to stop?"

"Well, I guess I thought I was jumping into a snowbank," I replied. The truth of the matter is I didn't think; my prisoner was escaping and

I reacted. As we drove into town, I thanked God again for watching over me as He had done so often before in the job He seemed to have selected for me to do.

CHAPTER XXII

A MAN TO MATCH OUR MOUNTAINS

I received a certificate of recognition for sustained superior performance of my duties as Deputy United States Marshal in the Fourth Division in December, 1965. The award was requested by then Attorney General Nicholas Katzenbach. I was deeply honored, but more so when Senator E.L. "Bob" Bartlett, one of the giants of his day in Alaska, and my personal friend, flew to Fairbanks from Washington, D.C. to present me with the certificate and a check for $500. I really felt I had served Alaska to the best of my ability in an era that was passing. I guess that is why I cherish this award more than some others I have received.

I had traveled the backcountry by dogteam, snowshoes, riverboats and airplanes, but I could see progress catching up with this young land I had come to call mine. I had faced dangers, had my life threatened, and made it through a lot of rough situations because I treated people as fairly as I could. Things were changing and this recognition ceremony caused me to reflect upon the changes more than I had before.

Law enforcement was not the only change I had to face when Alaska became a state. I really don't think I minded too much that my staff went from about 15 or 16 law enforcement people to my secretary of many years, Ethel "Babe" Lowell. I could accept change for I had seen Alaska come from the pre-World War II bush days into statehood, and now we were on the eve of the next rush, that for oil in the Arctic, which would eclipse all others that had preceded it. With the oil rush would come immediate, radical, perhaps traumatic changes which would vary markedly from those I'd coped with in the bush, but would resemble and outnumber those which I'd encountered in town. What would make law enforcement harder would be the cumulative impact of the subtle changes.

As a laxity began to invade our courts, enforcement became more and more difficult. Crimes were harder to prove and often we felt the criminal was more protected than we were. It was not unusual to see criminals we had apprehended back on the streets within an hour after we had taken them in.

When I became a Marshal in the Fourth District, I was responsible for the upper half of the entire territory from Barrow to Mt. Mckinley and the delta of the Kuskikwim. That type of "marshalling" ended forever with the new state system in effect.

I'd never been one to avoid a challenge, and as I viewed the preliminary rumblings of the oil rush I was glad that I'd made my retirement decision early. I'd already decided that I wanted to take advantage of what years I had left without stopping somebody's bullet because he was on dope, irresponsible or frightened.

The announcement of my retirement plans brought many friends forward to offer congratulations. Former U.S. Attorney Ted Stevens was now in Washington as one of our Senators. He sent this telegram:

Ted McRoberts has served Alaska as few men have during the last three decades. The help and guidance he gave me in Fairbanks when I was U.S. Attorney were typical of Ted's contributions to law, order and justice in our State. Ted was "The Man to Match Our Mountains", and I only regret that he will not serve for another 29 years.

Ted Stevens USS

I retired in June 30, 1970. I had enough sick leave coming to me to bring my total service to 29½ years even though I had gone to work in early 1943.

At my retirement dinner, I was presented with a poem spanning my years in Alaska. There may not be much poetry to it, but my friend said it expressed what they felt, and the newspaper printed it in the write-up.

"He came up to Alaska back in 1935,
Right away he loved the country so
to keep himself alive
he tried several different jobs
until he found the best of all,
it was working with the people
as a deputy marshal.

The year was 1943 that he finally hired on,
he was stationed out in Bethel
until trouble was all gone
so he moved up here to Fairbanks
and was soon Chief Deputy,
he has been here all these years
for this is where he wants to be.

Law enforcement was his hobby,
his vocation and his life,
he liked working with the people
and even in a time of strife
he was there to do the job
that he knew he had to do,
and he did it with distinction
and with pride and justice, too.

They all know him in Point Barrow
even Kotzebue and Nome,
He has traveled out to Rampart
to the Kuskokwim and Nome,
He has also been to Tanana
Fort Yukon and North Slope,
He has been throughout the Northland
even down as far as Hope.

Now the traveling that he had to do
was done in many ways,
He has traveled miles by dogteam,
on snowshoes and horse-drawn sleighs.
There were many miles by riverboat
by air and auto, too,
He always seemed to get there
for he had his job to do.

Now he's going to be leaving
for retirement and rest
Everyone of us will miss him
and for those who knew him best
they'll remember all the good things
that he did and things he said,
Yes, it's difficult to say farewell
to our friend and Marshal, Ted.''

Since those retirement days in the summer of 1970, I've wondered how I ever found time to work at a Marshal's job. I believe I have enjoyed what I set out to do in retirement as thoroughly as I did the years as a Deputy U.S. Marshal. I was reminded constantly that I would be bored with retirement after such an active life as a Marshal, but that has not been the case. I planned for retirement and that has made a difference. Using tour groups to solve my travel problems and save money, I have spent three weeks in Israel, a dream I had had since becoming a Christian in Takotna while still in the newspaper business.

The year after I retired, I toured England, Scotland and Wales. I saved enough money in preparation for retirement to buy a Dodge motorhome. I have traveled more than 50,000 miles in it including the Alaska Highway. I have put over 45,000 miles on it over Alaska highways. With the developing road system in Alaska, I have been among the first to travel them in the comfort of my motorhome.

Photography always interested me as a favorite pasttime. I have some of the best 16 mm films of life on the Kuskokwim, but I never had time to really enjoy photography before retirement.

Many said to me, "So you are going to retire and fish a little?"

My reply was always the same, "Well, it will be very little. I fished for so many years in the bush for survival, it will be no vacation now."

I plan to continue to retire as vigorously as I "marshaled" and enjoy what's left of old-time Alaska. Each year I take a trip outside to see my brother, Mike, in Idaho. Mike worked with me in law enforcement for many years and we are still close. I serve the First Baptist Church of Fairbanks as a deacon and find many fruitful and happy hours serving the God who cared for me so well during my career.

Alaska is changing and I'm able to watch it change. But the memories of 30 years as a U.S. Marshal during her days of growing up will never change, and I'm glad they were my years.

FINIS